A COMMEMORATIVE EDITION
LIMITED FIRST PRINTING

Rick Steber   Bonanza Publishing   Don Gray

Credits

Writing — Rick Steber

Photography & design — Rick Steber

Illustrations — Don Gray

Editing & typesetting — Kristi Steber

Scanart halftones by Wy'east Color, Inc., Portland, Oregon — Steven Fazzolari and Annette Lucero

Text paper, 80# Frostbrite, supplied by The Unisource Corporation, Milwaukie, Oregon

Photographs of Zola Lawrence, George and Lola Kennedy © Jerry Gildemeister.

Printing by Maverick Publications, Inc., Bend, Oregon — Gary Asher, Tom Healy, Ron Wells, Patricia Hammer, Denis Point, Bernice Rhodes, Jane Sampson, Warren Price and Bridget Wise.

Hardbinding by Oregon Bookbinding Company, Silverton, Oregon — Steve Kaufman

Bonanza Publishing
Box 204
Prineville, Oregon 97754

ISBN 0-945134-28-2 Hardbound Edition
ISBN 0-945134-29-0 Perfectbound Edition

OREGON TRAIL
LAST OF THE PIONEERS

Volume 2

HEART OF THE WEST SERIES

by
Rick Steber

Illustrations
by
Don Gray

BONANZA PUBLISHING . BOX 204 . PRINEVILLE, OREGON

DEDICATION

We dedicate this book to the memory of Lloyd Gray

FORWARD

West of the Oregon-Idaho border a brazen sun was making the bald hills shimmer. I walked along in the ruts of the Oregon Trail, daydreaming about Cold Springs, a famous camping spot; many pioneer diaries had mentioned the water, how sweet and teeth-rattling cold it was.

Each step kicked up dirt and it hung in the air. Behind me a dusty trail wove through stunted sagebrush. Warm water sloshed in my canteen. Cold Springs lay ahead, just a few more miles.

Afternoon slipped toward evening. Shadows lengthened. The punch went out of the day as the sun slipped from the sky into a pool of blazing gold and crimson. A lone meadowlark hurried to get in one last crystalline melody before darkness pulled a curtain over the land.

To the east the sky began to radiate a pale white light, growing stronger in intensity until a silver crescent peeked over the barren hill and pulled a plump full moon into the sky. I kept walking in the austere light but finally, bone-tired and thirsty, I gave up hope of ever finding Cold Springs. I lay down on the open hillside and pulled a wool blanket over me to ward off the cool that would certainly come before morning.

Sometime during the night I awoke to a pack of coyotes howling in a circle close around me. Overhead, stars like scattered embers were gleaming from a slate-black sky. And the moon was there, but a chunk was missing. I lay motionless, listening to the wild sounds, watching a distant shadow slowly consume the iridescent moon and, when it was completely gone, the coyotes quit howling and did not make another sound that night. *(Later I learned that irrigation wells ten miles away had caused the water table to drop. Cold Springs, such a landmark to the pioneers, no longer existed.)*

I walked the Oregon Trail from Fort Boise to The Dalles, a distance of nearly 500 miles, to gain a perspective of what the pioneers endured. I discovered that in many places the Oregon Trail is still visible. As I walked in the ruts, carved into the earth by wagon wheels and eroded by weather and time, I found many relics: horseshoes, ox shoes, iron rims, bits and pieces of wagons. Once, coming into the Grande Ronde Valley of Northeastern Oregon, at a spot where the pioneers had tied trees to the back of their wagons to act as anchors and rough-locked the wheels to slow their descent, I found ivory piano keys scattered down the steep hillside.

Hiking over the timbered ridges of the Blue Mountains the changing of seasons was evident everywhere; in the crispness of the morning air, the vibrant color of cottonwood trees lining the streams, the flurry of squirrels gathering food, and day and night the steady march of Canadian honkers passing high overhead, migrating south. Before long the tamarack would turn gold and the golden needles would release their grip. Snow would fall, build layer upon layer and push the deer and elk to lower elevations. The pioneers, not wanting to end up as the Donner party had, hurried through this section of the Oregon Trail and I did the same.

Below, on the broad sweep of the Columbia Plateau, Indian summer returned. I came to a field where a farmer was plowing under stubble. He stopped. We talked, chit-chatting about the weather, the lack of rain, the price of grain, the condition of the deer herd going into winter. He asked what I was doing. I told him, "I'm walking the Oregon Trail, following in the footsteps of the pioneers."

He wiped at the dirt around his eyes with a bandana, gave me the once-over and said, "Come with me, I've got somethin' ta show ya."

We walked through the freshly turned, ankle-deep earth to a pile of rocks. There was a tangled rosebush growing there, weaving in and out among the rocks, fighting to stay alive.

In a gravely voice the farmer said, "She was but eight years old. Died comin' out over the Oregon Trail." He paused, gathering himself, went on, "Before I took over, my father farmed this ground, before him my grandfather. We've always had enough respect for this grave to plow around it."

I stood there and thought about that little girl, thought about all she had seen on the way west: Chimney Rock, Scott's Bluff, Fort Laramie, Independence Rock, South Pass, Snake River.... She drank water at Cold Springs, was sick and probably riding in the wagon over the Blue Mountains, bounced and jarred across the rocky plateau. She had come so far, and died so near the end of the trail.

I tried to imagine what it would have been like when the end did come. Her father pulling back on the reins, stopping the team, setting the brake, climbing down, digging in that dry, unyielding ground with a pick and shovel. And then he went to the wagon, bundled his daughter in a quilt, carried her to her final resting place and laid her down. Dirt, a shovel at a time, filled the hole as the wife and mother, through her tears, read passages from the Bible and brothers and sisters carried rocks, piling them on top of the mound of loose dirt.

They stood for a time, each saying a sad good-by, and then crawled back into the wagon, continued on their way. Each turn of the wheels took them that much farther away from a little girl they loved so much.

I noticed little black marks on the lava rocks at my feet, realized they were tears, looked across the grave, to the farmer; he was crying, too.

At that moment the myth that had been the Oregon Trail in my mind was shattered. It was not the westward-ho version of books, movies and television but the story of people. People willing to forsake all they had, willing to pay the ultimate price in order to follow their dream of coming west and forging a new life.

INTRODUCTION

The route that became the Oregon Trail was developed by wandering mountain men. They followed buffalo trails across the plains, game trails through the mountains, and trails of commerce worn by Native Americans. Gradually a path of least resistance was carved from the Missouri River, the edge of the western frontier, up the Platte and Sweetwater rivers, over the Rocky Mountains at South Pass to the Great Basin and beyond to the Pacific Northwest and to California.

The eastern portion of the trail was well-traveled by fur company wagons supplying the trappers and traders at rendezvous. But it was not until 1832 that fur-trader and soldier-of-fortune Captain Benjamin Bonneville extended the road over the Rocky Mountains as far as Green River (Wyoming).

In 1836 Dr. Marcus and Narcissa Whitman and their missionary associates brought a two-wheeled cart to the Hudson's Bay Company post at Fort Boise (Idaho). Four years later the Reverends Harvey Clark and Alvin Smith, layman P. B. Littlejohn, and their wives brought wagons as far as Fort Hall (Idaho) where they were traded to a group of trappers.

The trappers pushed on but as the animals began to fail they lightened their loads and eventually discarded the wagon beds. Upon arriving at the Whitman mission they said they had made a mistake attempting to bring wagons through the Blue Mountains. Dr. Whitman told them, "Oh, you will never regret it; you have broken the ice and when others see that wagons have passed they, too, will pass and in a few years the valley will be full of our people."

News about the road west and the opening of the Oregon Country percolated in the East. Explorers and mountain men penned books of their wild adventures. Missionaries wrote letters and reports of crossing to the far side of the continent and their life among the Indians. They praised the mild climate, healthful conditions and the deep, fertile soil.

Ever since the Europeans landed on the continent they had, in fits and starts, pushed westward. But when they came to the Missouri River and the fringe of the broad, treeless plain, they halted. The frontier swelled with an influx of people. Between 1830 and 1840 the population of Missouri nearly tripled. Epidemics broke out: scarlet fever, measles, smallpox, meningitis and ague.

To the west was the Great American Desert and beyond that the Rocky Mountains. Many believed a wagon could never be taken the formidable distance to the west coast. But if they stayed on the frontier they had to contend with overcrowding, disease, and the economic hardships of the worst depression in the history of the United States.

In 1841 Missouri Senator Lewis Linn introduced a bill in the U.S. Senate that would encourage the settlement of the Territory of Oregon by extending "... one thousand acres of land ... to every white male inhabitant...." To many land-hungry farmers this promise of free land was like a pot of gold at the end of the rainbow. (The donation land law, giving 320 acres to each male citizen above the age of 18 and an additional 320 acres to the wife of a married man, did not become law until 1850.)

In May 1842 a wagon train consisting of 105 men, women and children, 18 ox-drawn wagons and a considerable band of horses, mules and cattle departed from Elm Grove, Missouri. At Green River some of the wagons were dismantled and used to make pack saddles. The remaining wagons were taken to Fort Hall where they were abandoned and the emigrants continued on horseback or on foot to the Willamette Valley of Oregon.

Historians recognize 1843 as the official beginning of the Oregon Trail. That spring a group of a thousand men, women and children, 120 wagons and 5,000 head of cattle assembled at Elm Grove, Missouri. When they reached Fort Hall some of the pioneers abandoned their wagons but others continued on to the Columbia River where flat-bottomed boats were built and floated through the dangerous rapids of the Columbia Gorge to the Willamette Valley.

The heyday of the trail occurred after gold was discovered in California in 1848. It is estimated one-quarter million people traveled overland to the diggings while another fifty thousand went to claim free farmland in Oregon.

The Oregon Trail was never a well-defined road running from east to west. It was a big, wide trail that followed the lay of the land with a series of landmarks serving as beacons.

On the open flats wagon drivers spread out so they would not have to eat dust from the wagon ahead. In wet years they were forced off the trail to skirt around bogs and marshy spots. But in some places natural bottlenecks forced the wagons into single file and there the iron rims wore deep ruts into solid rock.

Towns along the Missouri River — Independence, St. Joseph and Westport — had long been departure points for travelers over the Santa Fe Trail. It was natural that Oregon Trail pioneers congregate there to wait for the snow to melt and the grass start greening before they could jump off on a 2,000-mile migration to the promised land.

The early pioneers formed wagon trains for mutual protection and support. They outfitted themselves with teams of slow-moving oxen. The oxen — adult steers — were strong, could forage for food and were not likely to be stolen by Indians. They were driven by a man on foot controlling with a whip and voice commands and pulled wagons heavily loaded with personal articles, household goods and provisions for six months. They traveled at the rate of 10 to 12 miles a day.

Crossing the plains buffalo were killed and the meat cooked and cut into thin strips and dried. In the case of emergency some items, although expensive, could be purchased from fur-trading outposts scattered along the way: Fort Laramie, Fort Bridger, Fort Hall, Fort Boise and Fort Walla Walla.

In 1869 the transcontinental railroad was completed to California and in 1883 rail service reached the Pacific Northwest. At last emigrants could move west easily and quickly. But covered wagon pioneers continued to travel over the Oregon Trail. They continued for a variety of reasons: lack of money, a love to watch their work animals, a chance to go places where the steel rail did not reach, a sense of wanderlust — for all these reasons and more.

By the late 1800s the buffalo were gone. The Indian population, troublesome in the early days of the Oregon Trail, had been conquered and confined to reservations. River crossings that had taken the lives of many were spanned with bridges or ferry boats. Overcrowded camping areas, the spawning ground of diseases that took the lives of 1 out of 10 pioneers, were usable again.

The later-day pioneers no longer traveled in large wagon trains but in single wagons or small groups of family or friends. They were able to travel lighter because provisions and hay and grain could be purchased at scattered ranches or in towns that had sprung up along the way. If they ran low on money they could stop and work for a few weeks.

Instead of using oxen these pioneers switched to mules. Mules had sounder hooves than oxen and were faster, making 25 to 30 miles a day. Mules could be driven with reins while sitting in the wagon. Horses were also used but most men agreed that on the long haul, mules were more durable.

Historians tell us the Oregon Trail existed between 1843 and 1869. But wagon pioneers continued to travel over the Oregon Trail until affordable automobiles and a national highway system made the wagon obsolete in the 1920s.

In 1976 I met George Craig. As a six-year-old boy, in 1889, he had come west by wagon. George inspired me to search for others and over the past two decades I have sought out and interviewed 42 covered wagon pioneers.

As we celebrate 150 years since the first wagon train, all that remains of the Oregon Trail are ruts carved into the earth and a handful of people who remember coming west by wagon. They are the *Last of the Pioneers*.

1889
GEORGE CRAIG

e come west in 18 and 89. 1889. I was six years old. Rode a little white Shetland pony named Pet all the way. Uncle give him ta me 'fore we left outta Iowa.

Ah, Pet, he was a mighty good horse. Eat carrots right outta my hand.
Pet and me, we was like bread and butter. Lots a times, ta get outta the
dust, we'd ride ahead o' the wagon train but Pa'd warn me, say, "George,
you go ridin' away an' some bad guy is gonna knock you in the head an'
steal your horse." Nothin' ever happened – though I suppose it could've.

There was one night – see, we took precautions every night 'fore we
went ta sleep, like chainin' an' padlockin' our horses ta one o' the wheels o'
the wagons – but anyways this one night I was awakened ta the wagon
wigglin' ever so slightly. I tap Pa, tell him, "Shhh," an' he raises up real
slow-like, lifts the back flap, peeks outside, grabs holda his shotgun, points
'er, touches 'er off. Kaboom!

Turned out two men had sneaked inta camp, jacked up the wagon an'
was gonna steal the wheel in order ta get ta the horses. But when Dad
fired, they dropped the wheel an' hightailed it fer the brush.

We never knew who done it but always suspected Injuns, though
could've been white men. Out there in the middle o' nowhere white men
was no better'n Injuns, maybe worse.

Left outta Iowa in the spring an' it was fall 'fore we ever seen Seattle. We was a long time in comin'.

We settled on a little spread ten miles from town, stayed there the winter but the constant rain got ta Pa an' so the next year we started back fer Iowa. Ta pay the way we trailed a band o' wild mustangs.

It was Pa, Ma, an' sister Jane in the wagon with two or three horses tied on an' me drivin' the rest on Pet. Along the way Pet developed a kink in his neck, had ta be put down. I didn't want no one else ta do it; led him over a little ridge, said my good-bys, did it myself.

When we got ta Iowa we sold every horse we had fer $125 a head. That was a whole lot more'n we had in 'em.

I thought we was gonna stay in Iowa but Pa changed his mind. We started west, again. Even though we had been to Washington, hadn't liked it, that was the direction we was headed until the accident changed things.

Happened in the Blue Mountains. I was drivin' a wagon o' my own. Pa was leadin' in another wagon. We was on steep ground. His team took off. Don't know why. Mine followed suit. Ta save the outfit Pa overturned the wagon. I tried ta pull up but my horses threw their heads, kept runnin', tore my wagon all ta hell.

After that we went back ta the last valley we passed through, the Grande Ronde Valley. We settled there.

1891
CLIFTON ROSS

he most unusual thing about our crossing was the top buggy. It was probably the only top buggy to ever come out over the Oregon Trail.

We left out of Nebraska with two wagons and that top buggy. That was in 18 and 91. My brother John, five years older than me, drove one wagon; Father drove the other and Mother drove the top buggy with her sister riding along for company.

We used a team on the buggy because the ruts in the Oregon Trail were worn so deep that a horse by himself would be stuck up there on the middle.

The top buggy went first in order to keep out of the dust, but Mother made a lot of stops. Whenever we came across the site of a grave — and we were always coming across graves — Mother would stop and rearrange the rocks, piling them up. And if there was any kind of marker, a cross or board with a name, she would set it upright and pile the rocks to hold it that way.

When Mother was done she would catch up to us. She never got too far behind. She was afraid of being left out there alone.

I was nine years old, rode a little four-year-old gelding name of Logan all the way to Oregon. We had twelve other head of horses. On the way a mare foaled. We were several days letting her take it easy and waiting for the little fellow, so as he would be strong enough to keep up.

Some freighters overtook us and saw the mare and foal. They stopped us and asked if we were interested in making a trade. The railroad had come through that part of the country and forced them out of work. They were looking to trade mules and get in the saddle horse business.

Father gave up two mares and the foal for a pair of mules; one named Babe and the other Fanny. We put them on the wagon my brother drove. They were good mules and smart, too. My brother had a habit of falling asleep and if we were going downhill Babe and Fanny would move off the road to loose dirt to help slow the outfit some. Every time that happened my brother would come awake with a start. It was comical to watch.

I might have been young but I had responsibilities. Every evening when we stopped I had to help unhitch and tend to the teams. Another of my chores was to set up the tent and the cook stove and make sure there was wood for the fire. Mother and her sister slept in the tent and we cooked outside unless it was raining, then we moved inside the tent.

One time we traveled all day in the rain. I was cold to the bone and guess I fell asleep in the saddle. When I awoke I couldn't tell where I was — had no idea. But as it turned out Father had wrapped me in a canvas tarp, put me inside the tent, behind the warm stove.

I remember we camped on the main street of Boise, crossed the Snake River and turned off the Oregon Trail across the high desert of Eastern Oregon. We didn't see a soul from the time we left Boise until we hit the toll station on top of the Cascades.

We wintered on a farm in the Willamette Valley out of Brownsville and all of our horses died, even Logan. It was the alkali from coming across the Oregon Trail that killed them. If it hadn't been for the freight mules we would never have been able to farm that spring. Babe and Fanny pulled the plow. I suppose from all their years freighting they had built up a resistance and were immune to alkali poisoning.

1892
GRACE BYERS

We left Battle Creek, Nebraska hoping to reach Oregon before we ran out of money. It didn't work out that way. Coming through Wyoming we turned north and Dad looked for work.

Up along the Yellowstone River was the first time we saw Indians. A band of them came riding up to our wagons. Old man Whitcomb, the Whitcombs were a family traveling with us, was deathly afraid of Indians. He had heard so many stories and he thought they would scalp him. He crawled in back and hid under the bedding.

The Indians rode away but reappeared at evening camp and they brought along women and children. Old man Whitcomb stayed hid but we were friendly. Mother gave them food. One of them, I took him to be the chief because he was wearing a headdress made from eagle feathers, lifted a small Indian boy onto his lap and then gave the child to Dad.

I was only three years old but I remember quite well as the chief bent over me, scooped me up, held me on his hip. He smiled at me.

"Maybe we trade papooses," my Dad joked. But the chief did not take it as a joke – not in the slightest.

Holding me tightly in his powerful arms, he said, "We trade."

That scared Mother right now and she came and took me away. The Indians left camp.

For the next few days, until we got off the reservation, we were afraid the Indians might return. Later we ran into some settlers and they said we were lucky, that the last white folks who had tried to cross the reservation never came out.

Coming west Mother was always collecting pretty rocks she found along the way. Dad would come across them, fuss a little and throw them away, so Mother resorted to hiding places in the wagon.

One time, not too long after the Indian scare, a miner shared our camp. After dinner Mother decided to show him a few rocks, have him tell what they were. He was polite, examined each specimen, said what it was and never displayed any real interest until he came to a piece of quartz. He stared hard at it and demanded to know, "Where did you get this?"

For the life of her Mother could not remember — she had no idea. The miner asked questions and tried retracing the route we had taken. Mother still could not remember.

In the morning the miner was off in the opposite direction. And we were left trying to get a mile closer to Oregon.

Dad finally found work on a sheep ranch south of Bozeman, Montana. We were there several weeks and then tried to return to the trail but the horses were in sad shape. Dad sold them and the wagon. He used the money to purchase train tickets to Oregon.

The train stopped at every town and siding. At one stop a boy walked through the passenger cars selling paper cones of cherries. Dad motioned to the boy, paid him and handed me the paper cone and I ended up staining the front of my new white dress with bright red cherry juice. That is about all I remember of coming west.

1896
ZOLA LAWRENCE

There came a time when my folks could see no future in Kansas. And so one night at the supper table, Father announced we were going west. Friends had written us about Oregon, said there was no place in the world like it. Father said, "Guess we ought to give it a try."

I was only four years old at the time but I yet remember what it was like the day Father came home with a team of mules. He had traded our horses for them.

Mother said to him, "Why did you go and do such a thing?"

Father said he was only taking the advice of others, ones who had gone out over the Oregon Trail. He said they all claimed mules were better at foraging and, pound for pound, could out-pull a horse.

Mother was scared to death the mules would never make it. They were awful small. She tried to hold back the tears, could not, and cried and cried.

But there was no turning back in Father and in the company of my grandparents, two uncles, and one friend of the family, we headed west for Oregon. We had four wagons and the loose stock was herded along behind.

The trip, from my standpoint, was fun. Brother Percy and I played in the wagon. In the daytime Father took down the canvas cover so we could see out and put it back over the bows at night.

I only got into big trouble once on the whole trip. It came about one time we laid over a day so Mother could make bread. Father started a fire in the cook stove and Mother went about mixing the dough. But when she was ready to add the yeast cakes she looked high and low. Finally she came to me. I had eaten every last yeast cake. I got switched with a stick — oh boy! — and I didn't sit down for a month of Sundays.

Grandpa and Grandma Lawrence had horses on their wagon and there were a lot of times when one of them could not make it up a grade and our mules would have to go back and help pull.

Grandma had a nice little saddle pony she was fond of riding. Whenever she had a mind to she would ride; get away from the jostling or out of the dust. The rest of the time she rode in the wagon and the pony trailed behind.

But the day finally came when one of the workhorses gave out and Grandpa asked if he could hitch up the pony. How could Grandma refuse? To do so meant they would either slow us all down or they would drop behind.

Grandma stood as erect as a fence post, told Grandpa, "My little bay might have to do the dirty work, but he won't have my weight added. I will walk."

And she walked the rest of the way to Oregon.

The friends traveling with us fell in love with a little valley we passed through and dropped off. That was the last we ever saw or heard of them.

Our three wagons continued on. We crossed Snake River for the last time, turned off the Oregon Trail and headed due west across Eastern Oregon – straight into Indian trouble.

The Indians never came riding in, shooting and whooping, like you hear about. No, no, they snuck into camp in the middle of the night and stole every one of our horses. They left the mules. Guess they figured mules weren't worth bothering about.

There we were – three wagons and a pair of mules, out in the middle of nowhere. Father and one of his brothers went after the horses. They overtook the Indians, demanded the horses be returned. But the Indians refused, offered to trade horses for cattle. The Lawrences weren't fond of killing and so Father agreed and gave them a dry cow. After all, getting the horses was the most important thing.

Our goal was the Willamette Valley. And finally, after six months – the men were always stopping to work and earn money – we topped out at the summit of the Cascade Mountains. There was a gate set up at Soda Springs and a man was there collecting the toll. We did not have money to pay. All we could muster, among all of us, was a dollar and a half. Mother was terribly afraid he would make us turn around and go back.

But the old fellow at the tollgate said, "If you have come this far and only have a buck and a half, I'll be damned if I am the man to take it. Go ahead. Go through. The next man who can afford it I'll charge double. Good luck to you."

And that was how we came to Oregon.

1898
MABEL JONES

When I was eight years old my best friend was Grace. She was a Fitzgerald. I was a Jones, Mabel Jones from Hayes County, Nebraska.

Grace and I were the spitting image of each other.

Through the first and second grades we walked each other to and from school. Then came a morning when I was a potful of excitement and boiling over. I rushed up to Grace, threw my arms around her, told her, "Guess what! We're moving west. Dad said so last night."

Not until I saw the look on her face did I perceive the consequence of what I had said. We were leaving. Grace and I would be parting company.

In the days ahead there was precious little time for Grace and me. As we got ready to leave there were more and more chores to do but most every evening Grace and I got together, played out back.

One evening Mother told us children to set out everything we wanted to take with us in the wagon. We were down to the final stages of loading and according to Mother, weight was a prime consideration. Brother Alma had to dump half his marbles, Lawrence had to pick a single favorite rock. When my turn came Mother told me one doll was plenty.

The problem with taking one doll was that I had two, a china doll and a rag doll. I loved them equally well but the china doll had belonged to Mother and so I chose to take the china doll.

My parents allowed a certain amount of latitude with us children but the Fitzgeralds were another matter. They were very strict. Grace could not have a doll and her mother had even made her promise not to play with mine. But I could not just leave my rag doll and so I gave it to Grace.

"Mother would never let me have it," she told me.

I said, "Don't tell. Hide her in the willows. Make a home for her and when you play with her think of me, way out west, somewhere."

On the morning we were set to pull out there was a small surprise for each of us children. A gift from the folks. I got an autograph book, blue in color and just right for a pocket. I waited for Grace, wanting her to be the first to sign my book, coaxed her, "Please, then I'll have something to remember you by."

"Okay," said Grace. "But you have to promise. Do you promise?"

I nodded my head, asked, "What did I promise?"

"That you will not read what I write until after supper," she told me.

Grace took my autograph book and I remember her standing inside the house, the door was open, writing at the kitchen table. The chairs were tied on the wagon but we had no room for the table and so we were leaving it behind.

Dad called, said we had to go, said to get in the wagon. The neighbors were gathered to send us off and they called out, wishing us well and God's speed. I called to Grace, "Hurry, Grace, we're leaving!"

Our team, Flax and Floss, started the wagon with a lurch. Frantically I called to Grace. She came on the run, running as fast as her legs would carry her. The dust was boiling up, I was stretched out on the bed, reaching as far back as I could without falling over the tailgate. For just an instant Grace and I touched hands. Tears were streaming down her cheeks and she seemed so dreadfully sad. I caught one corner of the autograph book. Our fingers touched and then Grace could no longer keep up and she dropped back and was lost in the cloud of dust and the sea of racing children. One by one they gave up, stopped running and then we were alone. Completely alone.

All that day we traveled west. Finally we stopped. Dad unhitched the team, watered and rubbed them down. They were tired and relieved not to be pulling. A hole was dug for a fire and while the iron kettles were hung, so Mother could begin cooking. I gathered firewood. We all had to pitch in. By the time we had finished eating and the dishes were washed and put away, the sun was down and it was growing dark.

I went to the back of the wagon, dug down in a pile of quilts where I had hidden my autograph book and took it out. I sat down on the tongue of the wagon, opened my book and turned it so the light from the fire would fall on the open page. I read what my best friend had written:

> *When you get old and ugly*
> *Like young folks tend to do,*
> *Remember your friend Grace*
> *Is old and ugly, too.*

1898
MINNIE PFANNEBECKER

 ll the Pfannebecker children — two brothers, two sisters and I — were born in Iowa. We moved to Missouri but Missouri wasn't any good. Crops failed. We starved out. Dad loaded us into two wagons and without a cent to our name we started for Idaho.

Dad figured to work along the way. In Kansas we stopped and he worked in the harvest. There were a few other wagon emigrants camped with us. Their men were in need of work, too.

After a couple weeks Dad wanted to get traveling and he called for his pay. He hid it somewhere in the wagon. None of us, including Mother, knew where it was. Dad was the only one. Yet sometime between when he hid it and came back to check, the money was gone. One family pulled out right quick. Dad believed they stole it.

We existed on jackrabbits and sage hens. The menu never varied. Jackrabbit. Sage hen.

Coming across Wyoming, somewhere, the boys shot two sage hens and were sitting in camp picking and cleaning them when a big black dog appeared. He growled, showed teeth and in every way appeared to be ferocious. The boys threw him handfuls of feathers and entrails because they were afraid not to. Though complaining at the food given him, the big dog departed camp.

Next morning Dad was visiting with a farmer who lived in the neighborhood and he happened to mention, "We had a big black dog in camp last night. Acted real mean. The kids threw him sage hen feathers and guts. Know who he belongs to?"

The farmer responded, "Did he have a small white star on his forehead and long, matted hair?"

"That's him," answered Dad.

"Well," said the farmer. "That was no dog. That was a wolf. I'm surprised he settled for what he did. Must not have been very hungry."

It was late in September before we reached Montpelier, Idaho. By then our horses were so poor Dad decided to leave one wagon. Mother went through and sorted things. She kept very little of the wagon's contents. In the morning we pulled away, leaving behind my sister's doll. We didn't aim to leave it. It was just one of those things that happens.

Our destination was the Killmar homestead on the prairie outside of Grangeville, Idaho. Dad had gone to school with Mr. Killmar and other friends of the family lived nearby, the Segers and the Schraders.

The last camp of our journey was made in a treeless swale; rimrock showing through on the sidehill, a trickle of water down in the bottom and enough grass for the horses. It was a good camp.

Next day we made it to Killmars, only to discover the free homestead land was gone. If we wanted a farm we had to buy one.

Dad went to work with our teams and wagons hauling freight into the gold country: Florence, Elk City, Buffalo Hump. We endured the unpleasantness of our situation by looking down the road, to a time when we would have a place of our own.

Eventually, after two years of freighting, George Killmar got ahold of Dad, said a relative of his was homesick for Missouri and was giving up his homestead. Dad paid five hundred dollars for a quarter section on Big Butte, the highest point on the prairie. One side dropped off into Lawyer Canyon and the other looked over the Seven Devils country. The first thing we built was a barn. Dad always believed in caring for the stock first. Then there was a hen house, a smoke house and another barn strictly for the cows. We lived in the homestead shack for six years before Dad built us a house.

39

My last link to the Oregon Trail was Dick. He was my horse. A black gelding. He had come west with us. Nothing was too good for Dick. How I did love him!

I remember sneaking him grain, putting a few handfuls in with his hay, in order to fill out that little hollow spot on his hip. I loved him that much.

I went to school, grew into a young lady. And in the barn my sweetheart had grown old. I could no longer ride him. He could not bear my weight. And then he quit eating, would not even eat oats out of my hand. The end was near. It was so terribly sad.

One day a cousin came over. I sat on the back porch and watched it all: saw him, rifle in hand, leading Dick toward Lawyer Canyon. It was deep and rocky. We never had to bury dead animals, we always pushed them over into the canyon.

Poor Dick. Down to no more than skin and bones. I waited, waited some more, and then came the crack of a single shot. In my mind I saw Dick rolling over, and over, and over, and....

My cousin came walking back with the halter slung over his shoulder. He climbed the steps, paused to pat me on the head and without saying anything at all went in and had coffee with the folks.

THE TURN OF THE CENTURY

The dawning of the automobile era began in the late 1800s with steam, electric, and gasoline engines used to power "horseless carriages". At first these contraptions were confined to cities and towns because they were mechanically unreliable over long distances and because country roads were often impassable due to mud and snow.

It was believed that the automobile was nothing more than a passing fancy, a play toy for the rich. But in 1903 Henry Ford founded the Ford Motor Company and pioneered the Model-T, the first automobile to be made on an assembly line and affordable to the mass market. By 1915 the United States automobile industry was turning out nearly one million passenger cars and trucks a year and the federal government was rapidly developing a system of national highways. By the late 1920s the horse-drawn wagon had become obsolete.

The wagon pioneers of the twentieth century represent the last wave of the greatest voluntary migration in the history of the world. They traveled over stretches of well-worn Oregon Trail but in other places the trail had been plowed or was being replaced by roads and highways and the wagons competed with automobiles.

The pioneers reached their destinations. The work teams were turned out. They grew old and died in the pasture. The wagons, parked behind the barn or the woodshed, were soon overgrown by weeds and berry bushes. Wood rotted. Metal rusted. And in a world that seemed to spin faster and faster the last of the pioneers were all but forgotten.

1900
BERTHA "BIRD" SHADLEY

We never traveled the same road but we were wagon pioneers same as those who came out over the Oregon Trail in the early days of the west.

My family history goes back to Indian blood. Great-Grandmother was a full-blooded Pit River Indian. The story that has been handed down is that one day, when she was a little girl, the men were all away from camp hunting and a band of renegade Indians came in and killed everyone they could find. Great-Grandmother climbed inside a hollow log and stayed there, afraid to come out, until some white men happened along. One of them took her home, raised her as his child. She never knew her Indian name. She was always plain Susie.

I was born in Clear Creek, California. We lived for a time up to the Big Bend country, northeast of Redding. Can't rightly remember why we left out of there except that Mother had a sister, Aunt Eva, living in Portland, Oregon. They had been orphaned when they were young, hadn't seen each other in years. Mother wanted to visit her.

I think Father used that as an excuse. He was looking for better farm ground. I can recall him working on the wagon, putting up bows and stretching canvas over it, making it look like a real emigrant's wagon.

The day we pulled out, I can close my eyes and see Grandma — she wanted to come to Oregon with us so badly, she cried and she cried. And my two older sisters and Mother, who was pregnant with brother Lut at the time, they cried almost as much as she did.

Our team, Fly and Buck, regular workhorses, pulled our loaded-down wagon. A black hound dog name of Klondike went along for the ride.

Every time we came to a stream or a creek Dad would pull up, dig out his gold pan and wash a little gravel. He had wanted to go prospecting in Alaska but never got the opportunity. The closest he came was naming our dog.

I can picture Dad swirling the water and muck in his gold pan. Would he ever be happy when he found a little color! He would take the gold and put it in a vial. I've a hunch the gold he panned helped pay for our trip. We weren't wealthy people. If we had of been we could have taken the train.

47

One thing my mother insisted on, so us kids would have milk to drink, was to bring along a cow. Ended up almost killing Dad.

Milk cows were never intended to go mile on end. After a few days our cow got sore-footed, could not keep up and Dad built her a special set of shoes. When he went to nail them on, the cow kicked and a nail, only part-way in, ripped open Dad's hand. It bled bad, real bad. There was no stopping it. We were miles from anywhere, the nearest doctor days away.

Guess Dad would have bled to death if an Indian woman hadn't come into camp. She told us kids to collect spider webs, all we could, and to hurry. And so we ran through the forest, pulling cobwebs from branches. The Indian woman took them, packed Dad's hand and the bleeding slowed, finally stopped altogether.

Mother looked around, was going to thank that Indian but she was long gone and we never knew anything about her except she did save my father's life.

For a while we had a mule. My sisters and I would take turns riding, sometimes all three of us would pile on at the same time. One day a fellow came along riding a saddle horse and leading another. Dad always fancied himself a horse trader and, thinking he was moving up, traded our mule for the horse. The next morning when he tried to hitch the horse it kicked and fought and wouldn't let him near with the harness.

We kept that worthless horse until one day a farmer traded a silver pocket watch and a pendulum clock for him. It was a nice clock, ran real good, and coming down the road it would rattle and even chime on the roughest sections.

We crossed the Siskiyou Mountains and came to a spot where the train had plowed into a herd of milk cows. Cows were scattered up and down the track and some folks were out skinning them for the hides.

That was about where we turned off the main road and headed west. None of us had ever seen the ocean. Dad thought it pretty important we did and so we fought our way over mountains and came down along a switchback road that followed high above a creek in the bottom of a canyon. Finally came out on the great Pacific Ocean.

Not knowing about the ocean the first thing Dad did was to drive down on the beach. I suppose he had a mind to give us kids a thrill and dip a wheel in the water. But we got more than a wheel wet; for you see, we hit that soft sand and the next wave, an especially big one, dashed into us broadside. The horses shied, tried to go the opposite way. I was in back, scared to death, as we went up on two wheels, teetered there, and then it went over, flopping on its side.

I suppose Mother had a few choice words for Dad, about his hijinks, but I don't know that for a fact. I do know that every last thing we owned was wet. We spread what we could over bushes and driftwood along the beach. Even still it took several days to dry.

As we were coming up the coast Dad got a powerful craving for baked beans. Mother wasn't about to fix baked beans and so one night he cooked them himself. Several times he added water and then when we were ready to turn in — we slept in a tent — he packed coals over the pan.

In the morning he was raving about how great Navy beans were going to taste. He dug out the dutch oven, lifted the lid and there was a big, white snail on top. He must have poured it in with the water.

Mother asked, "You still have a hunger for baked beans?"

He shook his head, said, "Naw, my appetite is pretty well ruined."

I remember driving into Portland. We crossed the Willamette River on an iron bridge. Aunt Eva and her husband had a farm on the east side, close in. It was practically a ranch, it was that big. We turned Fly, Buck, and the milk cow loose in the pasture. They were in heaven. So were us kids. Being on the road wears a body down even if you are a kid.

Dad heard about work in Sherman County. He went up the Columbia on a stern-wheeler, landed in The Dalles and traveled to Sherman County where he worked in the grain harvest for Long-Hair Miller.

We went to visit Dad and he introduced us to Long-Hair. He was named for the fact he wore his hair braided down the middle of his back. He was a brother of Joaquin Miller, the famous western poet and writer.

Mother intended to return to Portland before her baby was born but he came early. Long-Hair Miller said that if the baby was named after him he would give him a colt. Mother made his middle name Miller. That old character never came through with the colt.

When Lut was nine days old Mother packed up him and us three girls and had Dad drive us to The Dalles. We caught a boat to Portland. We came back to the east side of the mountains only after Dad had located a homestead and put up a cabin for us.

Mother thought Dad was a little nuts for taking the homestead that he did. It was near Wamic and covered with scrub oak and rocks. And, of course, Mt. Hood was so close it seemed you could reach up and touch it. The cabin was a one-room affair.

It was November 19, 1900, the day Dad picked us up in The Dalles and drove us in the wagon the 50 miles south, through a snow storm, to our new house. A neighbor had come over, got a fire going, lit a lantern and the cabin, all lit up and warm, was something I shall never forget. Mother took a set of sheets and curtained off a bedroom for us girls.

It must have been a real hard winter; not much money, no canned goods, but the neighbors were real good to us. If the folks helped with butchering they gave them all the scrap meat. Mother would take lard and fix cracklin's which she put in cornbread. And we made hog-head cheese and used the jowls for bacon.

Come spring Mother planted a big garden. The neighbors gave her starts of everything: rose bushes, sage, blackberries. Dad cut down the pine trees and the scrub oak. He dug up the roots to loosen them and used the horses to pull the stumps. As soon as the land was cleared he planted it.

The old wagon that we came to Oregon in, we used that around the homestead for years and years. Finally we parked it and I suppose it rotted away to nothingness.

1900
LOLA KENNEDY AND GEORGE KENNEDY

Lola Kennedy

Dad was a roamer, always thought there was a better place just down the road, or over the next hill.

For a time we lived in Colorado but after a couple years it was off to Missouri. There were three of us kids and Mother was pregnant again. All across the plains it was mud, mud, mud and the horses were in such poor health that on hills Mother had to get out and help push. When Dad stopped to give the horses a rest Mother would catch up, lean against the wagon and clean her shoes with a stick.

That winter a baby boy was born and during the next two years there were two more. That made six. Dad had us constantly on the move.

We wound up back in Colorado; Dad working in the fields for a dollar a day and Mother making the same pay for cooking and housekeeping. She stayed with it two months, took the money, bought a cow. She felt it mighty important her children have milk and for a time we lived on nothing more than bread, milk, and butter we made by rolling cream in a half-gallon jar.

One day Mother received a letter from her sister. Aunt Josie and her husband were living out in Oregon and she wrote of green hills, wild game in the mountains, and said the mills were running and there was plenty of work for everyone. Mother was all for moving. And, of course, Dad jumped at the chance.

Several weeks before we left Monte Vista, Colorado, a burro wandered in to our place. He was old and had evidently been turned loose from a pack string. We adopted him, gave him the name Ned. Somehow we convinced Dad that we should take Ned with us to Oregon; that the older kids could take turns riding and thereby save our team. He was always a man who would listen to logic. He went and paid fifty cents a hoof to have Ned shod.

Ned was our pet, gray in color and stubborn as the day is long. He had one gait — slow — and there was no way in the world to make him hurry.

We departed from home on the first day of March, 1900 with a heavy wagon and a light spring wagon. John was to have the first ride on Ned and I was to have the second. After only a few miles it became apparent that Ned could not keep up. I hung back because I did not want to miss my turn.

The wagons continued on, passed over the horizon. John slid off Ned. He got in front, pulled on the reins, even put them over his shoulder and really leaned his weight into it. I stood behind, swatting Ned on the rump with a switch. But Ned refused to budge.

For a time John and I discussed our situation. Neither of us knew the way to Oregon. We had nothing to eat. No way of staying warm at night. What else was there for us to do except pull the bridle.

We ran mile after mile, after mile, finally caught sight of the wagons and it was a good couple of hours more before we overtook them. I remember sitting on the tailgate, choking on dust, looking back and thinking about Ned, out there somewhere, no bridle to hinder him, naked as the day he was born. Except for the brand new shoes.

George Kennedy

Comin' west we had to rustle for anythin' we got. The time I'm thinkin' about we was camped on the shore of a lake. After supper Dad glassed the far side with field glasses, spotted a bear, grabbed up his muzzle-loadin' shotgun and told us there was gonna be bear meat for everyone.

The loads he made extra heavy, maybe five inches of powder and shot, tamped 'em tight. The gun had two hammers; one barrel smooth, the other full choke.

We took turns with the field glasses, watchin' Dad make his way around the lake, easin' up on the bear that evidently had been shot at before because it would allow Dad to get only so close — just barely out of range — and take off, run for a ways, stop. Dad kept up the chase for quite a spell, came back pretty dejected-like.

The next mornin' we were headed out across an open flat and Dad spotted a sage hen sittin' on a rock outcroppin'. He was mighty anxious to get meat, we had been out several days. So he eased down from the wagon, got a few steps closer and touched off his shotgun. It was like a dynamite explosion. The force kicked him back, skinned up one whole side of his face and cracked the shotgun stock.

"God blame!" he says, pullin' himself to a sittin' position, "forgot them was b'ar loads."

I went to have a look at the sage hen. All I found were feet and feathers.

59

Lola Kennedy

Mother cooked over a campfire. Another of her chores was washing.
Every so often we would lay over for a day to rest the horses and Mother
would build a fireplace out of stones and set the smoke-black tub over it,
washing on a rub board with homemade soap. All of us children got in the
act — hanging clothes over brush. In some places, where the brush was
scattered, we might have clothes spread out for a quarter mile.

In order to save the horses all of us old enough to walk had to walk.
We went barefooted because Dad said we had to save our shoes for when
we got to Oregon.
I was thirteen, second mother to five younger brothers and sisters.
One of my nightly duties was to make beds in the wagons. The boys slept
in the light wagon and we girls in the other. Mother and Dad slept on the
ground.
We had come a pretty fair jag and had not seen a single Indian until
late one afternoon as I was making the beds a chill ran up my spine. I
turned around and not more than six feet away was an Indian brave,
wrapped in a blanket and sitting on a horse. I was scared, and for a
moment thought I might lose my footing and fall off my perch on the brake
block. The Indian saw I was frightened — he grinned, then rode away.

One evening we camped on a nice broad flat that had a stream
running through it. A string of forty-two wagons came into view. The
wagon master rode over, said they were on their way to California. He was
surprised we were traveling alone, beings we were in Indian country, and
asked if we had been having any trouble with Indians. We told him we
had only seen one Indian at close range.
They camped near us that night and in the morning, as they were

pulling out, brother George got kicked in the face by one of our horses. The shoe cut his face. One side of his jaw was completely broke and the other worked up and down. Terrible. Just terrible. And the wagon train bound for California went on its merry way. Didn't know anything about our trouble, wouldn't have cared, I suppose, if they had.

George Kennedy

I come into camp with an armload of firewood, wasn't watchin' where I was goin', walked behind one of the horses and she must have thought I was the dog 'cause she kicked, let me have it with both barrels. Knocked me over backwards, down a bank and into the river. Dad saw what happened. If he hadn't jumped in and saved me I would've drowned.

I don't remember none of it, I was unconscious, but I guess my face swelled up and I got the fever. We were 75 miles from the nearest town. Dad put me on a blanket in the shade beneath the wagon.

A few days later Mother was cookin' and an Indian come ridin' in on a cayuse, got off his horse, sticks his head under the wagon, looks at me with a rag tied around my head holdin' my jaw together. Without sayin' one damn word, he gets on his cayuse and rides away.

After a while a squaw wanders into camp. She takes the ax, chops a branch off a tree and then goes away, come back a little while later carryin' a whole stick full of flat leaf cactus. She held them over the campfire and burned off all the stickers. When she finished she made motions to Mother, and even though she didn't talk anythin' but Indian she got Mother to understand she needed rags. Mother tore up a bed sheet.

The squaw took a piece of the cloth, wrapped it around a few cactus and started pounding it with the flat side of the ax. When the cactus turned to pulp she came over and tied it around my jaw, then she went away.

About a week's time had gone by since I had been kicked and I had never come out of it. But a couple hours after the squaw put the poultice on my face I opened my eyes. Mother came runnin' over to me and wanted to know, "George, George, are you all right?" 'Course my jaw was broke, I couldn't answer.

The cactus worked so well that Dad didn't want to run out; he gathered a grain sack about half full and tied it to one of the wagon bows. When we finally did get to a doctor he said, "The best I can tell the jaw is set straight."

Mother explained about the Indian medicine. The doctor shook his head, told her, "Well, his jaw is improving. There's nothin' more I can do. I'd say go ahead and keep using the cactus."

And that was all the medicine I ever took.

Lola Kennedy

It was the Indian woman with the cactus who saved George's life. God bless Indians!

George had to drink soup and that sort of thing through a grass straw. His first real nourishment came when a farmer's wife fixed up a concoction of milk and eggs, sugar and nutmeg. We had to make him drink it.

The farmer said he could use a hand for a few days and promised us a place to camp, pasture for the horses, plenty of milk, eggs and such vegetables as they had. Dad took the job. We all welcomed the stop.

The farm was all but overrun with ground squirrels. The farmer's children had a job of killing ground squirrels and for every five tails they brought in their father paid them one penny. They asked if we would like in on the deal. Of course we were all for it.

The way we went about catching ground squirrels was to put a loop of twine over their burrow holes, wait for them to pop up and pull the twine tight. We had gathered a couple dozen tails when the farm kids noticed we were killing the squirrels. They were mighty upset, said, "Why did you go and do that? We just take their tails and turn 'em loose to grow another."

I would have been perfectly happy to have stayed on the farm forever but the wandering blood in Dad put us back on the road. His Oregon fever was running hot.

For me, the trip had lost its glamour. I was tired, ready to quit, settle down, have a home. One evening I saw a sundown where the sky turned just as red as you can imagine. I had read in the Bible about the world coming to an end, consumed by fire. I took it that the end was near.

After supper and chores I went to bed, tossed and turned before finally managing to fall asleep. Next morning the world was still in place. And we went on our way.

All across the desert country it was one dry camp after the next. Then one evening we topped a rise and came to, of all things, a lake. Even the dead-tired horses broke into a trot. But as we neared the shore we could see bones of dead creatures. It was a stark warning but we did not heed it. The horses plunged in, drank so greedily we had to pull them back.

And then we waded in and drank. The water had a rather strong taste and below the surface were scads of wiggly water dogs. When we filled the water barrel we were careful not to include any water dogs.

We all got sick to our stomachs from alkali poisoning but we did not dump the barrel. Out on the desert you can never predict when or where you might find water again.

Snake River was a blessing. The area was settled and we found pasture for the horses. At one farm Dad put up hay while Mother and us older children picked prunes. After the prunes were in Mother asked if we could have the summer apples that were going to waste. And so we picked and dried apples, seven flour sacks of apples.

It took us six long months to reach Elgin, Oregon. George's jaw was pretty well healed and we went to living in a tent behind Aunt Josie's place. We lived there all that winter and the only thing that kept us alive was milk, bread and dried apples.

1903
FLORENCE BOGGS

reat-Grandma and Grandpa Guerin were Oregon Trail pioneers. And so was Great-Aunt Susan. They crossed the plains by ox team in 1852.

Great-Aunt Susan wrote a ballad about their journey. The part that touched me most was when they were camped along the Snake River. Many of the company came down with mountain fever. Great-Aunt Susan wrote of that terrible time:

So then we buried two that day,
Two more were taken sick,
One of them was my husband dear,
I never can forget;

It seemed to me his dying words,
Are printed on my heart,
I could not think that he would die,
That we must forever part.

But, oh, his sufferings found an end,
August the second day,
Beside the little stream so clear,
Five of our number lay.

We loaded up and started on,
Which we were bound to do,
Leaving the spot on earth most dear,
Forever from my view....

Great-Aunt Susan was very special. She was a true Oregon Trail pioneer. Me, I came along too late to be special. Plain and simple, I was a wagon pioneer and nothing more.

I was born and grew up in the Willamette Valley near where Great-Aunt Susan and Great-Grandpa and Grandma Guerin took donation land claims, in the hills above what became the town of Silverton. It was lovely country.

I don't know why my father was inclined to leave such fertile land. Maybe he wanted to be on his own. Uncle George was partially responsible. He was a man who was never satisfied in one place for very long. He talked Father into moving onto homestead land the government was opening up in southern Klamath County. They decided to take adjoining desert land claims.

Mother was dead-set against going. She wanted to stay near her family. We had a marvelous place, raised lots of roses, had a big garden and many friends would stop to visit. But in that day women had no say. They did whatever the men told them to do.

I remember the going-away party for us. It was held on the first day of September and everybody in our corner of the world turned out. Just everybody. It was difficult telling friends and family good-by.

As sad as it was to leave friends I felt every bit as bad having to leave behind my cats. I had three momma cats and a passel of kittens. Father said he had enough to worry about just making the trip and refused to allow me to take even one kitten. I had to give them away. I was crazy disappointed.

Great-Aunt Susan took me by the hands, told me, "I know just how you feel. When I first came to Oregon I had to leave a lot of my things behind." And then she said, "I know how much you love your cats. I made something for you. Something very special."

She gave me a cross-stitching she had done of a cat, outlined in black and real, real pretty. After that I never saw Great-Aunt Susan again but I will always remember that look in her eyes. She knew what it was like to lose something or someone dear, wanted to spare me the pain. I couldn't keep myself from crying. Great-Aunt Susan dabbed away my tears with a handkerchief.

Uncle George and Aunt Annie started out the trip with a new wagon and team of horses. It was a big, heavy wagon. We had an ordinary wagon, the one we used on the farm. Father extended the sideboards, making it both wider and taller, put up bows and stretched canvas. It looked like a small version of an actual prairie schooner and was loaded with everything we would need to begin life in upper Langell Valley. We had tools, kitchen supplies, furniture and food.

My father drove the wagon and brother Lester rode with him. Brother Howard, eight years older than I, drove Mother and me in a two-seat buggy.

For company I had my rag doll with me. She was about a foot tall and actually she was two dolls in one; Arabella, a white girl with a beautiful dress and tipped upside down she became a black girl named Topsy.

We might have had a wonderful trip and ridden in style but one of our horses, a big red mare named Dolly, turned out to be sour. Father purchased Dolly a few weeks before we departed. He drove her a few times, had no problem. But late on the first day we discovered that when Dolly became tired of things, she'd just take off running.

Dolly was so big and strong that she dragged the other horse along with her. I remember Mother screaming and I suppose I was, too. Howard, he tried but could not hold her back. We went off the road, across a cleared spot and headed straight for a patch that had been logged off. There were big stumps sticking up and piles of limb wood. She could have tipped us over in a bad place and killed us all.

The buggy hit the first stump, bounced, came down, hit another and again went a mile high. All we could do was hang on and pray to the Almighty.

Hitting those stumps slowed us down some, enough that we got hung up, high-centered and wedged between stumps. And then Father was there, cutting loose the harness and it was over.

The runaway could have been far worse than it was. A few things were broken beyond repair; the doubletrees and the tongue, but the wheels were undamaged.

Father put Dolly and the other horse with his team on the wagon. He said that if she got it in her mind to run again there was no way she could drag three horses and the wagon. He made a trail wagon out of the two-seat buggy. Mother and I tried to ride there but it was near impossible because of the dust. The dust was awful. And so we rode in the wagon, sitting up on top of the bed. Howard rode with Uncle and Aunt.

Before long we established a routine for setting camp. When we stopped, even before the stock was cared for, the men would move the tin stove from the wagon to a flat spot. They would start the fire. And then it was the women's job to cook. The staple of our diet was what we called dough gods. They were made by mixing baking powder biscuits real thick and then dropping them on a hot griddle. That was our bread.

After supper and after the dishes were washed, dried and put away Uncle George would take out his violin and play and we would sit around the campfire and sing. When it was time to sleep Uncle George and Aunt Annie would go to the bed in their wagon. My brothers slept on the ground under the stars. Mother, Father and I slept in a bed in our wagon. Mother in the middle.

We had good roads as long as we were in the Willamette Valley but south of Eugene we started climbing into the Cascade Mountains. Here the road narrowed, weaved between towering fir trees and was rough as a cob with chuckholes.

It became clear that our horses were having trouble pulling all the weight. When we reached the town of Oakridge we went to the railroad depot, unloaded boxes and arranged to have them stored and sent to us when we called for them.

One night, near the summit, we set camp in a dry creek bottom. That was the only halfway level spot around. The place was littered with rocks, round rocks, big and small.

What happened that night I do not know. I can only go by what has been told me. But apparently I rolled out of bed, fell down between the canvas and the side of the wagon — it was roped down but not tight — and fell to the ground. I landed on my head, hit a rock, no doubt, and was knocked unconscious.

I remember gradually coming to my senses, hearing voices a long way off. I figured out it was Father and Uncle George discussing what they better do; Father saying we should return to Oakridge and Uncle George saying, "She'll wake up. She'll wake up." Mother crying, saying, "I'll get dressed. We must get her to a doctor!"

And I remember the light. It came from the lantern Aunt Annie was holding. I've still got it, saved it all these years. It was a harsh, white light. Faces, concerned and distorted, were there peering down at me; Aunt Annie, Uncle George, Lester, Howard, Father and Mother.

"She's coming awake!" shrieked Aunt Annie.

"Florence, are you all right?" Mother was asking.

I started to answer. My voice was thin like a ribbon stretched tight. "I think so," I told her and went on to add, "My head hurts."

Father had me squeeze his finger and wanted me to move my legs. Finally he allowed me to get off that cold, rocky ground.

The following morning my head still ached something fierce. Of course, we had to keep moving but at least I did not have to ride in the wagon. That kind of jostling would have absolutely killed me. Instead Mother and I rode in the buggy. It had springs and the ride was more comfortable than the wagon but, towed like it was behind the wagon, it was dusty as all get out and Mother and I had to tie bandanas around our faces in order to breathe. After a few days the headache all but went away.

We crossed the mountains and followed the old military road to Agency Lake. We saw the reflection of the sun on water a long way out and arrived just at dusk.

We were going through the routine of setting camp, had a fire started, when an Indian woman appeared from the brush that surrounded us. She was carrying two buckets and she held one up, said, "Dolla." Held up the other and repeated, "Dolla."

What she had were wild plums and so because they were fruit and we were hungry for fruit, Father gave her two dollars. We tried to eat them but they were too bitter. Later we discovered they were edible, and very good, if cooked with sugar. Lots and lots of sugar.

Skirting Agency Lake and Klamath Lake we came up and over the hill from Algoma country, came within a couple miles of the little settlement of Klamath Falls, but never stopped. Mother was anxious to reach the Young's place. As kids she had gone to school with Mrs. Young.

The Young family was living near Olene Gap, 12 miles east of town. We stayed with them two days and nights. Took baths in water heated on the wood stove, Mother washed clothes, got ahead some on baking.

Father and Uncle George had already filed desert land claims in the upper end of Langell Valley and we headed in that direction. The last town we came to was Bonanza. It had a big hotel, several dance halls and grocery stores. It was the hub and people from miles around came there for supplies.

We were better than 20 miles beyond Bonanza. And when we arrived there was nothing, absolutely nothing, on the property save for rocks, sagebrush, juniper, jackrabbits and rattlesnakes.

I remember Father pulling to a stop, saying, "Well, here we are."

It was absolutely quiet for a long moment, the only sound being the moan of the lonely wind, and then Mother made a wistful comment about what a pretty place we had left in the Willamette Valley, with hundreds of rose bushes, a big garden, family and friends. She turned to Father, "Gave all that up for this. You brought me here? What am I supposed to do here?"

After that we went back down the road a mile to the nearest neighbor, the Williams. Uncle George and Aunt Annie lived with them in the house. Aunt Annie did the cooking.

Our family moved into a wooden granary. It was a big, round, dank room with no light. Everything we owned was stacked in the room.

The wagons were used to haul rough-cut lumber from a mill on the west side of the valley to our claim. Two houses, made board-and-batten style, one for us and the other for Uncle George and Aunt Annie, were thrown together. We raced to finish before winter set in and we barely made it.

1906
SEDALIA RUCKER

y folks came west by train. They were looking to take a homestead and the only free land available was up in Northeast Oregon, in the Wallowa Valley.

I was born in Wallowa. Two years later Mother caught typhoid and died; three years after that Father passed away. There were eight of us children, no one wanted us all, so we were parcelled out, one here, one there. I went to the Rinehart family.

My brothers and sisters were never great about writing but occasionally I picked up news of what had become of them. My oldest brother took a harvest job over the mountains in the Walla Walla country. He drowned while swimming in a river. My oldest sister contracted TB and died.

The winter of 1904-1905 was a tough one. Mr. Rinehart, sick of the cold and snow, started talking about moving to a milder climate. When spring finally did arrive he took off to the Willamette Valley to look for a farm to buy.

It was about that same time that a young man came to live with us. His name was Bert Dexter. He was six years older than me. We fell in love and promised each other that some day we would marry.

Mr. Rinehart came home, said he had found a place and we left out of Wallowa County with a wagon all loaded down and a four-horse team. I rode a bell mare and there were six head of loose mustangs. Bert helped me with the herding.

The first day we kept going until almost dark and reached Tollgate on the top of the Blue Mountains. The old fellow who lived there let us use the barn. We slept in the hayloft.

Next morning we were on the road early. We came out of the mountains and dropped down and hit the old Oregon Trail outside of Pendleton. The going was rough, loaded with chuckholes, on account of the farmers hauling wagons of wheat over it.

We were one day to Echo, three more to John Day River. For the time of year the flow of water was high. Bert took the bell off my horse, tied it around his saddle horn and led the mustangs into the current.

I waited to make sure he was safely on the other side before I entered the river. My horse was short-legged and I had to hold my feet in the air to keep from getting wet. I never had a bit of trouble and neither did the Rineharts in the wagon.

We had just started up the grade out of the canyon when Charlie, our dog, commenced to barking. I looked back and he was on the opposite side of the river. Charlie had a habit of riding in the wagon and whenever it would stop he would jump down and scout the neighborhood. That was what he had done when we came to the river. I watched as he leaped into the current and swam, just his little head sticking out, and when he reached our side he never even bothered shaking off, he just ran for us.

Upon reaching The Dalles we loaded everything aboard a big stern-wheel ferry. It was like nothing I had ever seen— a boat so large!

Passing down the Columbia Gorge it started raining and it rained all the way to Portland. We docked, unloaded and Mr. Rinehart found a livery where we left the horses and wagon. We walked uptown, took rooms in a hotel and ate at a Chinese restaurant. That night we were all stricken with stomach sickness.

The next morning Mr. Rinehart insisted we continue. It rained every mile of the way and it wasn't until well after dark before we pulled into Yamhill. We went on through town, past the last house where warm light shone through the windows, and started climbing into the foothills.

Mr. Rinehart had a relapse of stomach sickness. Bert took over driving the wagon. I was left alone, bringing up the rear, in darkness so absolute I couldn't tell what the end of my nose was doing. Cold rain poured down by the bucketful. The wagon creaked and each hoof pulled loose from the mud with a loud smacking sound. Wheels splashed through puddles. The horses kept in communication with an assortment of nickers and whinnies. I followed dumbly behind, trying to crowd the horses toward the feeble lantern light swinging back and forth on the front bow of the wagon.

We started up a grade and apparently I was pushing the mustangs too much because all of a sudden Mr. Rinehart yelled, "Get out of here!" But it was too late. One of the mustangs had gotten in the way of the wheel horse and she had gone down. Mr. Rinehart and Bert unharnessed the animal and helped her stand. When we finally got underway again Mr. Rinehart reprimanded me with, "Keep 'em back. Don't crowd 'em." And I did as he said.

The wagon finally rolled to a stop in a little orchard and the team put their heads down and started chomping apples. By then I only had one horse with me, that was Bert's saddle horse. The rest were scattered up and down the road, feeding their bellies.

Mr. Rinehart did not have a key to the house and had to break in the front door. There was not a stick of furniture inside and I remember how forlorn it seemed with the lantern light shining on empty rooms. But there was dry wood in the woodshed and Bert lit a fire in the great rock fireplace.

Then Bert and I went out, unhitched the team and put them away in one of the two huge barns that were on the property. Then we rode back down the road to round up the mustangs. Bert rang the bell; mustangs nickered, some from quite a ways away, and they came on the run. We brought them to the barn, rubbed them down and put hay and grain in the manger.

By then it was midnight. Bert and I were soaked clear through to the bone, cold and tired. We went inside and the Rineharts had it warm. It seemed cheery, almost like home.

That night we slept on the hearth in front of the fire. Little did I know that three years later, standing in front of that great stone fireplace, Bert and I would be married.

1912
MAUDE MOSIER

ear as I can tell the Mosier family has always had goin' in their blood. Great-Grandpa immigrated to America from Germany and Great-Grandma came from France. They were on the east coast for a while, then moved to Nebraska, after that it was on to Iowa and then back to Nebraska.

All his life Grandpa Mosier had lived near the Oregon Trail and had watched pioneers passing through in covered wagons. He was always talking about loading up and heading west. Finally he talked his son John, my father, into making the trip. Probably didn't have to talk too hard. Father was a rambler, might have come to the Pacific coast on his own. He was a great hand to travel.

Grandpa and Father were the best two men in the country, bar none. I can say that because it's true. Ain't nobody ever come close. They were hard-working, true to their word and like I said, they were curious about what was over the next ridge.

Father arranged to lease our ranch to neighbors, Guy and Goldie Syckles, for one year. We spent all that spring pulling together an outfit. Needed three wagons; one was our farm wagon, and we purchased a spring wagon and a lumber wagon. Fixed them up with bows over the top and heavy canvas covers that would shed the rain, protect us from wind and dust storms and give us a measure of privacy. There were shelves built inside, cupboards and beds, too. Father bought and traded for mules and horses, choosing animals that were strong and dependable. He purchased axes, saws, hammers and tools with which he could work on the wagons.

Mother pulled together the kitchen needs: heavy kettles, large skillets, granite tableware, coffee pot, bread pans, cream cans for water jugs, camp stools, tents, kerosene lanterns, candles. We cured hams and bacon, set aside bags of beans, potatoes, canned food and lard. Made a supply of lye soap. Purchased quantities of sugar, flour, salt, pepper and baking powder.

Even had a first aid kit. It contained turpentine, camphor, liniment, aspirin, cough syrup, rolled bandages and a tonic made from sulphur and molasses.

Before we left, out of the clear blue, Web Longacre asked me to marry him. He was a neighbor, thirteen years older than me, one of the nicest fellows a girl could ever hope to find. He and I went to dances all over the country. We could waltz, two-step, square dance and even do the fancy dances like Waltz Vienna. "Can you dance the Oxford?" "Yes, you bet I can...." I thought seriously about marrying Web but Grandpa was dead set against it. He told me, "You're only 17. You're too young to get married. Make the trip with us. If you love him and he loves you then you'll have the rest of your lives to spend together."

Grandpa made me stop and think. I wanted to get out in the world, see what was there. I wanted to wash my feet in the great Pacific Ocean. In the end I told Web he would just have to wait.

One thing I took special care with was my traveling bed. Figured if I was comfortable sleeping it would go a long ways toward an enjoyable trip. Sewed two comforters together, lined one side with a warm blanket and canvas on the other so it would shed water.

As the time for our departure drew near friends and even people I hardly knew would come up to me, warn me about how wild the West was and warn me about the Indians, said they could attack at any time. That kind of talk made me laugh. I would tell them, "Indians are human, too. If I treat them like friends then how could they be anything but friendly?"

On the 4th of June, 1912, at 10 a.m. our caravan of wagons departed Mosier Ranch in Banner County. Nebraska. Wagon number one was pulled by two brown mules and driven by Father. Mother rode with him and the wagon was loaded with bedding, clothes, water cans, oats and baled hay. Wagon number two was driven by my brothers Archie and Bert and pulled by two mules, a white and a gray. Their wagon contained the cupboards, food staples, clothes in suitcases and the hunting rifles, a .22 and a .410 shotgun. I drove the third wagon. It was pulled by two horses, Fred Gilman and Sox. We carried the pots and pans, dishes, kerosene stove, tents, nose bags for the horses and dry goods like sugar, flour and potatoes. Grandpa was my passenger. He was age 73. Also had along two saddle horses, Dick and Brownie.

We traveled along the North Platte River; Scotts Bluff, Torrington, Fort Laramie, Casper. It was west of Casper that we left the river and headed cross-country.

At first Mother did the cooking but her knees went stiff on account of arthritis and she couldn't get up and down very well. I took over.

The kerosene stove was set up in my wagon and I could cook there out of the wind and the weather. But after having learned to cook with wood the kerosene stove scared me to death. It popped and cracked and puff-puff-puffed so bad I figured it was dangerous, threw it out of the wagon. After that I cooked over a campfire.

Grandpa was crazy about fishing. Before we left home that was all he would talk about, saying, "Out west they've got great, big fish. Nobody fishes. I'm gonna catch me a mess like you can't even imagine."

Grandpa carried fish line and a hook in his pocket and every time we came to a trickle of water he would break a limb off a tree, catch a grasshopper or some kind of bug or worm for bait and try his hand at fishing.

Along the way someone told Grandpa the best fishing in the whole wide world was in Yellowstone Park. I remember sitting around the fire and Grandpa begging Father, "They say Yellowstone is one of the great wonders of the world. Lot of real interesting things. Ain't too far out of the way. How about it, Son, can we go?"

Father was always one to investigate new country and so just before reaching the Wind River Indian Reservation we swung north off the Oregon Trail. At Thermopolis we had a soak in the hot springs and that was quite a wonderful experience.

Made it to Cody, visited where Buffalo Bill lived, then swung due west into the mountains. Climbed to the 8,541-foot elevation through Sylvan Pass, battling snow where we had to riprap the trail with limbs and branches to get our horses and wagons through the deep drifts. Reached the east entrance to Yellowstone Park where the ranger sealed our guns so we would not be tempted to shoot game animals.

We took our time traveling through the park. Grandpa was always going off fishing. He would come back, bring his stringer of fish to me. I was his favorite. Don't say that to brag but it was fact. He would hold his stringer and exclaim, "Well, whatdya think of these?" And then he would want to know, "This be good country to stay in. Well, wouldn't it?" And no matter what I was doing I had to shake my head that yes it would be grand to live in such a bountiful land.

Grandpa was used to catching catfish, ugly fish, but in Yellowstone he was catching big, native trout. He was in seventh heaven. Absolutely in seventh heaven.

Traveled along, seeing thousands of hot springs and mud pools, cliffs of black glass and petrified forests. Old Faithful was about my favorite. All around there the ground sounded hollow. The part I did not like were the bears. They were nasty and anything in the way of food had to be put away.

Left the park through the west entrance and the rifles were unsealed. The boys, if they saw wild game, shot it. They killed ducks, grouse, sage hens and rabbits. They would bring it to me and while Grandpa drove I would dress it so the meat would be ready to cook when we stopped.

Dropped down out of the mountains toward the high plain that bordered the Snake River. Wherever we could, we camped in meadows with creeks and plenty of big timber. The stock would graze, Grandpa fished, the boys gathered wood and I cooked on a grate over a campfire. If it rained or was cold we ate in the tent. Baked biscuits for every meal and a cake every now and then. Did the laundry with a washboard in the stream. Picked wild berries. Bought vegetables, eggs and milk where we found them, but out there ranches were few and far between.

Reached Snake River and passed into a lava field where there was a cabin. On the door was tacked a note reading, "Come in. Make yourself at home. Leave things as you found it." We were mighty appreciative of the roof over our heads and a floor beneath our feet.

Crossing the lava field the following day was rough going. We camped and you could look back, see the cabin and nearly throw a rock to it.

At Pocatello we rejoined the Oregon Trail and followed it along to American Falls, Twin Falls, Boise and forded the Snake River at Payette into eastern Oregon. Again we swung away, this time to explore the John Day country before swinging north again and rejoining the Oregon Trail near Pendleton. It was outside of town where we camped for several weeks on property owned by an Italian. He was farming, raising produce for the market and Dad and my brothers worked for him bringing in the crop. He had a large flock of white geese he used as weeders in the fields. One day they got into our food tent and really made a mess.

Frank Nudo was a hired hand there. He took quite a fancy to me. It had been a good long while since I had attention paid to me like that. I didn't encourage him but I didn't discourage him, either. When we pulled out Frank rode many a mile with us. Father was more than a little upset. He asked me, "Has your suitor decided to join our family?"

Next time Frank rode over to be near me I asked him exactly what his intentions were. He said, "I want to marry you." I told him I wouldn't have him, that I didn't want him, that I had a beau back in Nebraska who was waiting for me.

Took him a few more miles to realize my mind was made up and I wasn't going with him. Then he turned his horse around, headed back. He went his way. I went mine.

At Umatilla we drove the wagons onto a freight boat. The horses and mules were put below deck in the hole. If memory serves me it cost Father $300.

I rode on the deck, had the grandest time of my life; no lines to hold onto, no jostling wagon, no dust. We floated along down the mighty Columbia River without a single care in the world. At Celilo we drove the wagons around the falls and loaded them on another boat, a ferry that took us to Portland.

Portland was the largest town I had ever been in and, of course, I got myself turned around, lost, and was sitting on a corner bawling my eyes out when a gentleman comes up to me and says, "Can I help you?"

"I don't think so," I wailed.

"What's the problem?"

"I'm lost."

"Don't worry about a thing. I know every street in this town and I'll take you wherever you wish." And so I quit bawling, went with him and in a few minutes he had me standing in the lobby of our hotel.

After sightseeing around Portland we returned to the road, headed south to the upper end of the Willamette Valley. We wanted to cross over the coastal mountain range and get a look at the Pacific Ocean but the rainy season had arrived and Father decided we should find a place to winter. He found a house to rent and pasture for the stock in Lynx Hollow, near Cottage Grove. We settled in for the winter.

Spring of 1913, bound and determined to finally lay eyes on the Pacific Ocean, we started our wagons for the coast. Our first view came at Winchester Bay. For the longest time none of us said a word as we stared off at the curved horizon where the thin, gray line of ocean met the gray sky.

Camp was set near two old men who said they were trappers. They had been fishing and gave us a salmon. Grandpa could not believe that a fish could be so huge. He was beside himself, saying over and over, "I just can't believe it."

It was too heavy for him to carry, all of 40 pounds, and so I ran a rope through the gills and packed that mighty fish on my back to our camp where I cooked it over the campfire. We had quite a feast. Grandpa said he was a lucky man on two counts; that he got to see a fish so big and second that he had the enjoyment of eating it.

We lived on the beach for several weeks. Got acquainted with an Indian family. They taught us many things: where to pick berries, and where and how to dig clams, catch crab, fish in the ocean. They had a girl about my age and size. For fun I tried on her dress. It was made from buckskin. She and Mother painted my face and took a photograph of me. I did, somewhat, resemble an Indian.

The coast was such a wonderful place and Mother Nature so giving that Father inquired about the price of land. And to my shock and astonishment he up and traded our three covered wagons and eight head of horses and mules, as well as our camping gear, for 320 acres on the Winchuck River, a house and a small barn.

He said about the place, "It's truly paradise; got salmon in the river, wild game in the hills, range land, tall timber, how could we go wrong?"

I was madder than mad. Plain furious. And I up and called Father a bad name, a really terrible name, right to his face. He sputtered and spit, kicked in the sand with the toe of his boot, said, "You're speakin' pretty plain, ain't ya, gal." Even to this day, and I'm 99 years old, I am embarrassed about the name I called him.

But try driving a team from Nebraska to the Pacific Ocean, you can't help but get attached to them. Fred Gilman and Sox were like part of the family. I patted them, loved them, and would call them my "honeys". I'd ask, "Do you want Momma to pet you?" and they would nicker and stick out their heads so I could rub their necks.

Never knew which one I loved best. Loved them equally. Of the morning I would always brush them, curry comb on their hip where the harness rubbed, talk baby talk to them. "Momma is going to rub your shoulder. How do you like that? Do you love your Momma?" If it was Fred Gilman or if it was Sox he would turn his head and look at me, telling me yes. And they could whistle, actually make a whistling noise when they wanted my attention. I could ask if they were hungry and they would nuzzle my hands to see if I had any rolled oats or other treats.

The other animal I truly loved was the gray mule, Syckles, named after our neighbors Guy and Goldie Syckles. If Syckles thought he had the upper hand he would try to get away with it. Never could trust him to stay in one place unless I hobbled him.

Once I forgot to hobble Syckles and he took off for Nebraska on the run. Even with hobbles he could make two or three miles of the night if he had a mind to. That old fool! I caught him, climbed on him bareback, whacked him across the hind end a lick or two and made him run all the way back to camp.

I remember standing on the porch of the Winchuck place watching our wagons head down the lane. They broke over the ridge, went out of sight. One of the horses whinnied. That was it. They were gone. I stayed around a few more weeks. Then caught passage on a ship to San Francisco. From there I rode the train back to Nebraska where I married Web Longacre.

1913
IRMA SELLS

Susie was my love. She was two-foot tall, had a china head and a body filled with sawdust. She had the prettiest green eyes. They would close when I laid her down. My baby Susie.

I was an only child and she was more like a sister than anything. When Father had his appendix burst, and through the operation, I held onto Susie. She helped pass the time.

One day while Father was recovering, I rushed to Susie with really big news. We were moving. Father said so. He and the butcher at the market next door to our house, Billy Osborne, had come up with this wonderful idea — taking a covered wagon to California. And in order to pay for the trip we would haul along a motion picture projector and show silent movies in the towns we passed through. Most rural folks at that time had never seen motion pictures and would undoubtedly be willing to pay for the privilege. Mother was very sensible and she said a wagon provided barely enough room for supplies and traveling gear. The idea of dragging along a projector was quickly discarded.

Billy and his wife Anna had a one-seat Maxwell but automobiles were more or less a novelty. Taking it to California was never considered. We could have gone by train but according to Father and Billy that was no way to see the country. So Billy traded the Maxwell for a wagon and two mules. Their names were Edna and Jennie. I held Susie and told her, "We really are going."

The day we departed, May 22, 1913, we had a big send-off from relatives and friends of the families. I think most everyone in South Omaha was there for the occasion. A photographer took our picture and then we pulled out. Billy walked. Father drove the wagon and Mother was on the seat next to him. I sat in the wagon with Anna. She was very upset. She did not have any children and all her maternal instincts had been directed at a parrot she kept in a cage. She could not bring the parrot and I think she resented my Susie nestled on my lap and my mongrel dog Rover beside me. I watched as the crowd got smaller and smaller, then we rounded a bend in the road and they were gone from sight.

The wagon had been built for comfort. It had wishbone-shaped springs under the box that rocked us like a cradle and would creak and groan in response to the uneven road.

That first day, despite our late start, we made 22 miles, reached Waterloo and set camp near the bridge that crossed Elkhorn River. I thought we were really out in the world. I had never been so very, very far from home.

A routine was quickly established; late in the afternoon we would find a camping spot and if it were near a creek Dad and Anna would go off fishing, they loved to fish, while Mother and Billy would set up the tent, start a fire and fix supper. After eating and the dishes and pots and pans were washed, sometimes, if they weren't too tired, the folks and the Osbornes would sit and play cards.

The most difficult part was breaking camp. Usually we were up by five, then it was fold the bed clothes, pick up the hay that served as our mattress, fold the tent, cook and eat breakfast, feed and water the mules, pack the wagon, hitch up and get ready to go. I would sit on the wagon seat between Mother and Father and would be so sleepy. Mother would allow me to put my head in her lap and sleep a little extra. Billy walked, rode in the back with Anna and sometimes he drove the wagon.

For the first few days the road was tolerable but sandy in stretches and hard on the mules. In the afternoon the wind would come up and the sand would blow, sting our skin, make it hard to breathe and unless you squinted it would blind you.

We started out with an oil stove but it was more trouble than it was worth and Mother discarded it, choosing to cook over a campfire. Another item that proved useless was a folding screen. We took it along to give the two families a measure of privacy. We got rid of it. If you wanted privacy you went out behind a rock or a bush.

A week out from South Omaha, a few miles west of Grand Island, we saw our first long-eared jackrabbit. In fact, we saw jackrabbits all over the place and were soon counting on having rabbit for supper but Billy missed every shot. As we got ready to camp a storm came rolling over the prairie. It looked like we were going to get wet but it only sprinkled a little. The wind blew, which in a way was good because it kept down the flies and mosquitoes, which were quite a nuisance.

At Kearney, a busy little town, we stopped for supplies and continued on through the heat of the day, praying that a gentle rain would fall, cool things off, settle the dust some. At Lexington, which we reached on Sunday, we had an extra special treat, ice cream. I had wanted to attend a movie but the town was very pious and did not allow movies to be shown on the Lord's day.

Billy purchased a fine table in Lexington. He brought it to camp and we had our first meal around a table. For chairs we used boxes and kegs.

The following day we lay over on account of the heat and the fact Father was not feeling well from the after-effects of his appendix operation. His back bothered him. The time was used to wash clothes and write letters to family and friends back home. Near where we camped was a farm house and the woman who lived there, feeling sorry for us I suppose, brought over an armload of lettuce and radishes from her garden.

From Lexington we battled a storm. The wind and rain won out. We had to lay over again and when we did start up, the road was muddy and in spots nearly impassable.

It was in this stretch where Rover began thinking it was up to him to put food on the table. Whenever Father or Billy reached for a rifle to shoot a rabbit Rover would jump from the wagon, commence barking and running around. He would chase rabbits but he had about as much success actually catching one as the men seemed to have in shooting one. Father became quite peeved with Rover's antics and declared the next time he jumped out of the wagon he would shoot him. After that, whenever a rabbit was spotted and Father reached for his rifle, Mother or I would reach for Rover and hold him in the wagon until after the shooting stopped.

The main crop grown along the North Platte River was alfalfa. The farmers were friendly and generous toward us even though there were quite a few travelers on the road, most in covered wagons like us but a few in automobiles.

Anna spotted the first prairie dog of our journey. Before long we were passing prairie dog towns of considerable size. I was fascinated how the cute little things would sit upright on the edge of their homes, only to disappear and pop up again like the clown in a jack-in-the-box.

Rather than sit on the wagon seat or in the back with Anna, I took to walking. Mother was worried about me walking but if the truth were known I would often sit on the step at the back of the wagon and hitch a ride. Our road followed the railroad. I amused myself by waving at the engineers, thought myself wonderfully successful if they waved back.

We cut across a corner of Colorado and managed to eat breakfast in Nebraska, dinner in Colorado and supper once again in Nebraska.   It was near Julesburg, Colorado where Rover actually caught a prairie dog. On close inspection it somewhat resembled a rat.

The farther we went the more spread out the towns and farms became. One night we could not replenish our supply of hay and had to feed all we had to the mules. That night, rather than using hay for a mattress, we slept on the ground. Father's back pained him terribly.

The country changed from wide open prairie to bluffs, sometimes steep, and pine trees every now and then. Evidenced by the many abandoned houses and homesteads, it was tough country to make a living.

A mighty storm overtook us and we were forced to make a quick camp out in the open with no protection. We tried to out-wait the storm, the folks played cards to pass time, but finally we had to continue on, fight the head wind and rain. We found an ideal camping spot near a creek and a farm but the woman who lived there came out and told us to move on. And so we pulled up the tent, moved down the road a couple miles.

On the 14th of June we neared the Wyoming border. At Bushnell Station we bought a tin of sardines and were sorely disappointed. Instead of being a special treat they tasted like they had been soaked in coal oil. We passed through a herd of sheep, the first we saw on open range.

After passing Pine Bluffs we dropped back onto the prairie and there were very few trees. We were straining our eyes for the distinction and reward, an ice cream cone, to be the first to see the Rocky Mountains. Father won. Off in the distance, a hundred miles or so, could be seen the faint outline of mountains.

There were acres and acres of pretty wild flowers and not many people to share them with. We did manage to spend one night near a ranch. The woman of the house came to our camp and brought her daughter with her. She was about my age, a little older. When she heard we were going through Cheyenne she became very excited. Evidently, for her, going to Cheyenne was a major event and she explained in great detail about how we could pick up our mail at the post office; that we would go through swinging doors to the General Delivery window where a man would stick out his head and ask our name.

We reached Cheyenne, went to the post office and it was just as she described. There was mail for everyone except me. I sat on the steps and cried. I said I was disappointed I did not get any mail but I am sure that homesickness was catching up with me, too. We went to a motion picture show and that seemed to help my disposition.

One month out of South Omaha we started up into the Rocky Mountains. We thought we had climbed a long ways but we were told by

105

a man we met that we had barely begun. We passed prospector diggings and the country was bare and desolate. That night we heard a mountain lion scream.

In the morning the mules fought the harness. One of them kicked Billy. But, as always, the mules were hitched and we got back on the road.

We dropped down to a high plain. On one side were snow-capped peaks and on the other the mountains were covered with evergreen trees. Upon reaching Laramie the newspaper man stopped us, asked some questions and said he was going to write a story about us. I guess it was unusual to have wagon pioneers passing through Laramie.

We continued on a long, tiresome drive, coming across a pair of auto goggles along the road but no automobile, although it was evident from tire tracks that one had passed that way. Late in the afternoon we reached a desirable spot to camp with plenty of grass and water. A group of sheep men were camped nearby. We were told that the company had 175,000 head of sheep scattered out over the range. Nearby they were shearing sheep. There were 27 shearers. One man sheared 208 sheep that day. At eight cents a head he made good wages.

For the next several days there were no towns, no farms or ranches and we ran out of bread and had very little other food to eat except for the rabbits Billy and Father managed to kill with their rifles.

We were still 15 miles from Medicine Bow, it was hot, the ground baked hard as cement and the road in tough shape. Billy shot at a rabbit but only wounded it. It squealed and when it did Rover squirmed from my arms, jumped down and gave chase. The rabbit ran down a hole and Rover continued in pursuit, digging and squirming his way downward. We waited for him to crawl out but he did not. Finally Father said we had to be on our way. But I was not about to leave Rover. I called his name, over and over, pleaded with him to come out but he stayed put. Even

Father and Billy got in on the act; Mother, too. Anna was the only one who did not try. She stayed in the wagon, out of the sun.

"Load up," directed Father.

"We can't leave him out here!" I cried and put up such a fuss, along with a few tears by Mother, that Father was forced to give in. He and Billy used shovels to dig down to the bottom of the rabbit hole. Here they found Rover, clenching the wounded rabbit in his teeth and wagging his tail as if to say he deserved all the credit.

We reached the town of Medicine Bow. There were two large hotels, three general merchandise stores and a saloon where, according to Father, a customer could purchase a glass of beer for 15 cents or get two for a quarter. We had dinner at one of the hotels and continued on. The country was nothing but sagebrush and grease wood as we climbed into the mountains. We crossed the summit and reached Carbon, an abandoned coal town. The buildings were empty; store, opera house and all the rest. The coal must have run out.

At camp that night two wagons pulled in near us. The people came over to visit. They were from Illinois and had been on the road for three months. They were very generous and gave us a bale of hay for the mules.

In the morning we were away early. It was cold enough to frost and we wore jackets until nearly noon. When it did warm up the mosquitoes came out and knowing full-well their days were numbered, attacked with a vengeance.

For the next several days we endured the cold, the bugs, and a road so rough we were forced, at times, to get out and walk. Added to this was the lack of food and water. To satisfy our hunger a biscuit dough was made, but since we had no oven the dough was cut into strips and fried in grease in a skillet over the campfire. It was delicious.

One fearful night was spent on a lonely, open flat devoid of grass and trees. A wind storm struck us and nearly tore up the tent. Mother and Anna and I sat in the corners and hung onto the canvas for dear life while Father and Billy worked to keep the mules from running off. The poor beasts were being pelted by sand.

After that sleepless night Father's health deteriorated rather rapidly. We reached Green River and the doctor took one look and said that he must be taken at once to the hospital in Rock Springs.

Father had contracted a case of what the natives called mountain fever. We never knew how he happened to get it but the doctors said he would be laid up several days.

It was decided that the Osbornes would continue on and that when Father was fit to travel we would take the train. A week later, in Evanston, we rejoined the Osbornes and continued our westward trek.

I suppose the time we spent in Rock Springs softened me to the rigors of trail life because the first day back on the road I threw a temper tantrum. What happened was I was awakened early. And then I wanted Anna to sit up in the front on the seat between Father and Billy so I could stay in back, put my head in my mother's lap and sleep some more. But Anna refused. I reacted by jumping from the wagon and walking back the way we had come.

"Come back here," called Father. I ignored him. "Irma, come back here this instant!" Still I ignored him.

He saw that it would take drastic measures and he stopped the wagon and came after me. He gave me a spanking right there in the middle of the road. A man was working in his field near the road and he yelled at Father, "Stop beating that girl."

Father was riled up enough that he challenged the farmer. "You come over here and I'll give you some of the same." But the farmer stayed where he was.

The mules were also in a balky mood. We came to a mountain stream, it was only a few feet wide, and they refused to cross it. The men tried every conceivable form of persuasion from coaxing with handfuls of hay and grain, to beating with a stick, to actually building a fire under them.

Finally a make-shift bridge had to be fashioned with sacks of sand before the mules would cross. After that they had the bluff in. Any time Father saw water up ahead he would get those rascals running and they would be over it before they had the opportunity to balk.

We passed through a spot called Devil's Gate where the rocks crowded in close to the road and then rolled into a broad valley where orchards were growing amidst fine fields of grain, tomatoes, potatoes and even strawberries. As we neared Salt Lake City the road became as smooth as pavement and was lined on both sides by towering shade trees. We spent the night camped in the feed yard near the center of the city and not far from the Mormon Temple which we visited the following day. I listened to a recital and was absolutely awed by the enormous auditorium and the deep, rich tones of the pipe organ.

We were told the trip over the Sierra Nevada would be difficult and so the grown-ups were determined to sell our outfit and go the rest of the way on the train. We had several fellows ask the price and waited around, hoping one of them would come back, but they never did. And so we pushed on, headed around the north end of the Great Salt Lake and then turned west.

For quite a ways the road was littered with scalped rabbits. A bounty of five cents was being paid and every man and boy in the country had armed himself with a gun. Father shot eight rabbits in a very short time.

We came across a ranch and the people traded us some eggs and more shotgun shells for our rabbit ears. Billy killed the first rattlesnake we had seen on the trip. We skirted the Grouse Creek Mountains and crossed the border into Nevada near Montello, a railroad town.

We cut through rolling hills and across sagebrush flats where there was not a living thing to be seen for miles and very little grass for the mules. The road was so hilly and rocky that in places we unhitched the team and pulled the wagon by hand because we thought the wagon might tip over and did not want to damage the mules.

When we finally reached the Humboldt River the going was easier and there was grass for the animals. We reached Elko, a town of 2,500 with a courthouse, some nice stores and many saloons.

After that it was uphill, downhill, across valleys and canyons. Wherever there was water the mosquitoes would torment us and torment the mules. We could retire to the tent but the poor mules, the only relief they got was when we tied sacks over their heads.

At one point we met travelers in an automobile. They were coming from California and said they had been on the road for five weeks. They said they did not much care for California. I guess not everyone considered it the land of promise.

We stopped at Battle Mountain, a very lively mining town. Nearly every other business was a saloon. We had dinner in town but while we were eating our mules disappeared. We looked high and low for them before finally discovering they had been taken to the livery barn. The sheriff had picked them up and if we had had any money he would have pinched us, but as it was he let us go without a fine.

West of Battle Mountain the country was so barren not even a jackrabbit would live there. It turned out we were on the wrong road and had to double back.

     As we neared the town of Winnemucca a man driving a Model-T Ford came up behind, did not see us, I guess, and ran into the back of our wagon. The impact broke one of the bows and tore a hole in the canvas cover. The man was very apologetic, gave Father a dollar, said, "This should pay for the damage," and went his merry way. We were tickled to death to have the dollar.

That was the same day I turned eleven years old. I got a box of candy and a spanking for good measure.

The next morning we were away early. The road was sandy and hilly. We took turns walking to lighten the load as much as possible and on the worst grades we got behind the wagon and pushed. We ate dust all day and camped in the dust. It was like that for several days running.

In Reno we stopped and had the luxury of a shower. Back on the road we met a man and woman traveling from California, trading horses as they went. They said that there was no place as good to live as California. They told us about a schoolhouse ahead where we could camp and so we went there. We slept in a shed and put Edna and Jennie in the barn.

We followed a tolerable road to Carson City, meeting several automobiles as we traveled. From there on the road was sandy, winding and in places nearly straight up until we reached the summit where we found a wonderful camping spot, an abandoned cabin, barn and spring.

The following day we started down and had not gone far when we spotted Lake Tahoe. It was like an emerald glittering on a bed of evergreen. A more beautiful sight I never expect to see.

We drove through the forest, spent the noon hour near the lake allowing the mules to graze on the abundant grass. Continuing, we passed many summer resort cottages. We stopped at a livery barn and had to pay

$1.50 for a hundred pounds of hay. Later a shower overtook us. It became a heavy downpour that dampened our spirits. We pitched our tent, started a big bonfire and even though other wagons and a few automobiles continued to travel we stayed where we were and endured our introduction to California weather.

Fourteen weeks since departing South Omaha found us at 7,000 feet elevation in the middle of the Sierra Nevada. We descended to near the American River where rocky formations were like shingles laid one on top another. The road was a boulevard, wide and well-packed.

Upon reaching the town of Placerville the man who operated the store gave us the privilege of camping on a vacant lot. And in the morning we were away early. The road was terrible with dust being six inches deep and everything we owned covered with it.

As we dropped to the valley floor the country gradually changed from pine trees to oak trees and finally to nothing but dry grass. In Sacramento I saw more automobiles than I had ever before seen in my life. We did not waste time, the folks and the Osbornes were eager to get to our destination.

We passed through Hayward and from there on in the country was pretty much settled. We found a vacant lot in the middle of Oakland and set camp there. All around us were people coming and going and a city bustling with every-day life.

I remember a "For Sale" sign Billy Osborne tied to the bows of the wagon. He wanted to sell the outfit for a fair price but horses and a wagon were not in demand and he had to let it go for next to nothing.

The last night we were camped in Oakland Father and Anna were off someplace and I was playing. I went racing into the tent to get a bonnet for my doll Susie and when I threw back the flap there was Mother in the arms of Billy Osborne. It might have been perfectly innocent but it was quite a shock to me. They stepped away from each other quick-like. Mother busied herself patting down her apron while Billy muttered, "I better...." He stepped around me and went outside.

The following morning Dad, Mother and I took an apartment on 22nd and Telegraph Avenue. They did not allow pets there and even though it broke my heart we had to give Rover away. Mother found work as a matron in the gymnasium at the University of California at Berkeley. Father was not so fortunate in finding a job. The only trade he knew was as a cooper and making wooden barrels, like the horse and wagon, was on its way out. Another thing working against him was the ill feeling against outsiders. Those who had been born in California or lived there a long time banded together into a group called the Native Sons. They would make it hard on anyone hiring an outsider. Eventually Father did find a job washing dishes in a restaurant but that was the best he could do.

I remember him complaining that California was not the land of milk and honey he thought it would be. Not long after that we returned to South Omaha, this time traveling on the train. Susie rode on my lap.

As far as what happened to Billy and Anna Osborne I don't rightly know. I suspect that after spending so much time together, traveling all that way in a covered wagon, that everyone had enough of each other. All I can say is — they went their way, we went ours.

1915
CHARLES THOMPSON AND RALPH THOMPSON

Charles Thompson

There were five of us kids in the family. Each born in a different state.

Dad was nothin' more'n a gypsy horse trader, a happy-go-lucky sort. Never raised his voice or his hand in anger. It was up to Mom to use the switch when necessary. She was strict as sin.

I could never understand why Mom would marry a common horse trader. She was from a high-class family. Imagine they met at a dance someplace. Picture I have of 'em from back then shows Dad was a nice-lookin' fellar. He played mouth harp, called square dances. Figure they met at a dance an' she fell in love.

Mom would henpeck the ol' man somethin' fierce, henpeck him up to a point. When it come to providin' a livin' Dad made the decisions. He done all right. None of us ever went to bed with an empty stomach.

Dad heard 'bout free homestead land out in Wyomin' an' was able to wrangle a contract with the government to provide remounts to the cavalry. So in '15 we pulled up stakes in Nebraska, we were livin' in a sod house, an' headed our wagons toward Douglas, Wyomin'.

We had a hay wagon, called it the camp wagon, that Mother drove. It was a big, wide-body affair, with a canvas cover over the top. We had most everythin' we needed: grub and gear, kitchen supplies, wood cook stove, an' a bed for the folks and my sister.

Dad drove the trap wagon. It was loaded with hay, oats, horseshoes, harness an' the like, things needed for the horses or the wagons. Us boys usually slept out under the stars on top of the hay in the trap wagon.

We had eight head of workhorses, good workhorses, go a ton apiece. An' Dad trailed up to a dozen trade horses. Back in them days, before tractors come along, farmers liked to have matched teams an' Dad made sure he had a horse of most every color in his string. When he made a deal he usually got a better horse than he gave, an' cash to boot.

Dad took a hardscrabble homestead out there in the open country of Wyomin' an' went to buyin', tradin', breakin', an' sellin' horses. After a couple years he was ready for a change. A rich lawyer Dad had become acquainted with through horse tradin' asked him to run a ranch for him in Colorado.

So again we loaded our wagons, headed down the road. This time I was old enough to drive an' traded off drivin' the camp wagon. It had springs under the bed an' rode nice an' easy. When I wasn't drivin' I'd be ridin' my burro. That durn burro, I could turn him loose an' he would stay with us, tag 'long like a pet dog. All of us kids could ride him, an' did, takin' turns, but Dad couldn't ride him for love nor money. If he couldn't buck Dad off he'd lay down an' roll him off. We had many a good laugh at Dad's expense.

Dad never had much patience with my burro. Once in a while it would get into the trap wagon, put his nose in the grain sack an' steal oats. The old man give him the devil for it.

The thing that burro absolutely refused to do was cross a bridge. 'Fore I got him somebody must have dumped him through a bridge. I always had to swim him.

At one point we come to a long bridge. The water was too wide an' the current too strong. I told my burro, "Guess this is where you an' I part company."

We crossed over, traveled a few more miles, set camp. Just before dark I made the rounds, checkin' the horses, hobblin' the ones that needed hobblin', an' what did I find — my burro! Gave him a hug. How he crossed that river has always been a mystery to me.

One time we were camped 'long the road on an Indian reservation. We had a dog name of Coaly, a black mongrel. Normally he was a pretty good watchdog. An Indian come into camp, threw Coaly a chunk of meat, said, "Humph, him fat dog. Him good to eat."

All night I was worried the Indian would come back, steal Coaly. In the morning Coaly was there, sleepin' under the wagon, but the horses, even my old burro, were long gone.

Dad straps on his .44 hog leg, picks up his .30-30 rifle an' his shotgun,

takes off afoot. Goes maybe a mile an' a fellar, drivin' a brand new Dodge tourin' car, pulls up, wants to know, "Where are you goin' with all that fire power?"

Dad tells him, "Someone stole my horses. I'm gonna get 'em back."

"Hop in," says the fellar. "I'll give you a lift."

They go a ways, top out on a ridge, an' there on the back side are the horses, tied as neat as you please to sagebrush. Dad unties 'em, brings 'em back. He never saw an Indian but we always figured they tied off the horses, got out of there when they heard the car acomin'. That was about the only trouble we had with Indians. By then the Indians that was left was pretty much tame.

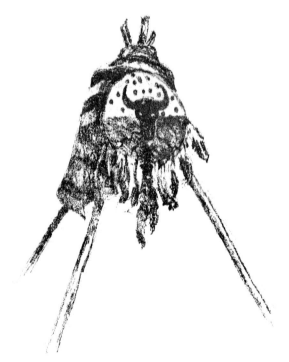

Dad kept his shotgun an' his rifle at the ready. Any time he spotted a rabbit, sage hen, grouse, or pheasant he would shoot. He was a crack shot, pop their heads right off an' never hurt an ounce of meat. Soon as he made a kill he stopped an' took care of the meat. 'Cause of the huntin' Dad usually took the lead with the trap wagon. When we come to a ranch, ranches was scattered an' you might not run 'cross one for twenty or thirty miles, he would drive in, try to buy a bale of hay or two an' a sack of rolled oats or barley. He always fed his horses good, kept them in tip-top shape.

Rarely did we come 'cross an automobile. We didn't pass through many towns and automobiles mostly kept to towns. They stayed close 'cause no one was goin' in somethin' as undependable as an automobile. Why they didn't even have pullin' power! Come to a halfway decent hill an' they turned 'round an' backed up it.

A few times we had run-ins with what I call buggy cars. They were the ones go "putt-putt-bang-bang" down the road. Scare the horses. Never had a runaway but come close.

We made it to where we was goin', up in the high mesa country out of Ridgeway, Colorado. So high up we were only one valley away from where the Rocky Mountains began. We moved onto the lawyer's place an' started in farmin'. Dad had me workin' from sunup to sundown.

I was nine years old the first time I ever pulled six lines. I could plow an acre a day, two if I was lucky. It was all dry land, wheat and taters. Raised some nice taters. Had 1,029 acres. When it's all said an' done, I was a man without ever gettin' to be a boy.

Ralph Thompson

My brother Charley shot me. We were living up on the mesa.
Happened this way. I was out playing in the barn the way young kids do,
up in the hayloft. Charley had a BB gun, was shooting at birds. Shot me
instead. Hit me in the left eye. Oh, did it hurt! I let out a scream. My
brother and sister helped me down and took me to the house.

Charles Thompson

Out back was an old log barn. One day the young kids was playin'
out there, I was thinnin' out the bird population with my BB gun, an' my
brother Ralph sticks his nose in the crack 'tween the logs 'bout the time I
pull the trigger. The BB hits that cotton-pickin' crack, ricochets.
I didn't even know I'd hit him 'til he gives out a yell that'd curl paint.
He was hurt bad. We got him down an' put him in the wagon. It was my
wagon. I had bought it with my own money. Saved up for it. Cost nine
dollars in the hardware store in Montrose. I pulled the wagon. Sister
Freida tried to comfort Ralph the best she could. Other than that one
scream he never cried or nothin'. An' it never bled. Momma took him in,
washed the eye an' that was 'bout all could be done.

Ralph Thompson

One day at school, we were outside at recess, a covered wagon comes
up the road. It was pulled by an old mule and a skinny brown horse. They
stopped in front of the schoolhouse. It was the rattiest outfit I ever laid eyes

on, piled high with washtubs, boxes, loose clothes. As we gathered around four kids drop off on the far side and peer at us through the spokes of the wheels.

The fellow that was driving asked, "Could any of you tell me where the Thompson place is?" Well that was a shocker, that they should know our family. It turned out they were the Keudell family and we had been neighbors back in Nebraska.

Us kids paired off. Jack and I were best buddies. He had lost an arm and me with my blind eye it seemed natural we should be friends.

Jack had a sense of humor, even for a kid, and there wasn't anything the two of us wouldn't try. I remember one time Jack and I fashioned rifles out of limbs. We tied bandanas across our faces, hid beside the road and waylaid one of the neighbors. We jumped out from our hiding place, leveled our sticks at him and Jack told him, "Your money or your life." He gave us each a quarter.

That evening I was showing Charley the money and Mother overheard. She made Jack and me hike all the way over to the neighbor's place, apologize and give him back the quarters.

If there was anything that was out of place, any little thing that happened that could not be explained, Jack and I would get the blame. We were like two peas in a pod. I suppose most of the time we deserved whatever we had coming.

Charles Thompson

The Keudells took a farm near us. But the old man was never a farmer, he was a bookkeeper. Didn't know the first thing 'bout farmin'. All he had was that mule an' the horse. How could he hope to make a go of it? From the day they landed it was only a matter of time 'fore they starved out.

We stayed on the mesa a year or two an' then Dad got tired of the snow an' sixty below. We moved down on the flats to a dairy farm. Come the spring of '23 Dad said he wanted an even milder climate, said we were goin' to Oregon.   I think he just had itchy feet, wanted to get back on the road an' trade horses.

Our outfit consisted of a new Studebaker wagon, made it the trail wagon, an' the same hay wagon brought us from Nebraska to Wyomin' an' from Wyomin' to Colorado. We fixed it up, made the box eight-foot wide an' twenty-foot long. There was a bed 'cross the front where the folks an' my sister slept and' us boys slept on a straw tick on the floor. The canvas flap on the front end could be tied back. I would sit on the bed to drive.

A number eight cast iron stove was bolted to the floor an' the stove pipe ran up through an openin' in the canvas cover. In the mornin' Mother would start a fire an' get the ham, hotcakes, biscuits an' eggs cookin'. We would feed an' harness the teams, then come in, eat, go back out, hitch up.

By the time we was ready to go the dishes were washed an' put away. At the end of the day Mom could get a fire started before we stopped. That saved a lot of time.

Within a few days of headin' out, we were settin' up camp one evenin' when a black family with four kids pulls up in a brand new Cadillac tourin' car. They was from somewhere back east. Drove clean 'cross the country. The fellow comes over to Dad, says, "We've never been in the mountains in our lives. We're scared to death of cougars. Would you have any objection if we camped close to you?"

Dad told him, "It's a free country. Camp wherever you like."

That night, several times, our dog Coaly barked at the coyotes. Just to make the city folks feel at ease, Dad fired off his shotgun.

The black family traveled with us the next day, the Cadillac wadin' through the mud but when we hit snow it was worthless. We hooked onto 'em, pulled 'em through. After we started down the west side, the road wasn't much more'n a cow trail but the Cadillac could travel faster an' the black family went on their merry way.

Ralph Thompson

We traveled from Montrose to Grand Junction and on toward Salt Lake City. We could ride in the wagon if we wanted but most of the time we walked or hitched a ride on one of the horses.

I think we had 16 head of horses when we took off. That number fluctuated, especially as we neared Salt Lake City. We traveled slow so Dad could work trades with the farmers. They were always eager to trade and try and upgrade their team or match them better. It was a thing of pride for them to have matched work teams.

We might stop at noon, unhitch and it would be my responsibility to herd the horses along the road so they could graze on the free grass. With our big wagon and the horses we were kind of a novelty. Folks would travel to see us and work a trade with Dad.

Charles Thompson

Dad always dolled-up his workhorses. He could take a fifty-dollar horse an' turn him into a five hundred-dollar horse with a few pretty things: tassels, spreaders, silver bells.

We come into trade alley at Salt Lake City an' you could hear people talk, "Look at those pretty horses a'comin'." I was drivin' two teams, matched bays in the lead. They were mirror images of each other, in looks an' how they held their heads an' worked together. You couldn't tell one from the other. They were buggy-type horses, small. Too small for our needs. Sure enough a fellar snaps them up, trades a big bay horse and gives two hundred dollars to boot.

It was a good trade for us. The little bay team would play out on me every day. They were not big or heavy enough for the long haul. I hooked the big bay up on the wheel, not in the lead, 'cause I didn't know what kind of an animal he was and wanted him on the tongue where I could control him. On the lead you don't have much control. If they want to tangle you they can tangle you bad. Turned out that big bay was one of the best horses we ever had.

From Salt Lake City we headed north and west into Idaho. There weren't many folks out there on the desert. Once in a great while we would meet a freighter. He would most likely be pulling two or even three trail wagons an' be workin' teams of up to sixteen jackasses. I called them jackrabbits 'cause they only went maybe 600 pounds but one of the freighters explained it to me, said, "Small mules can travel almost as fast as a horse. An' they're tougher than a horse. Where a horse is particular 'bout what it eats, a mule'll eat most anythin'."

Traveling through that country was rough on our stock. There were times we would be miles an' miles from water. When we came to a dry stretch we traveled at night, keep right on goin'. Dad would say, "A horse is not near as apt to die on his feet," an' we would take a rag, wet it in the water barrel and rub their nostrils.

One time, out there in the middle of nowhere, we broke a wheel. Wasn't no way to fix it. The old man takes it off, goes an' cuts a limb from a green tree, fastens it to the wagon an' the axle with a log chain. Made a skid. We traveled that way for better than a hundred miles. Every so often, when the skid wore down, we would jack up the wagon an' drop down the skid to where the wagon was level. We went through a half-dozen skids, maybe more. When trees were scarce we borrowed fence posts. Finally we came to a blacksmith shop an' the smithy fixed the wheel.

Ralph Thompson

We passed through Burley, Twin Falls, Boise, and crossed the border into Oregon. West of Pendleton we were overtaken by a Model-T Ford, overloaded, kids hanging on as best they could. I remember my surprise when I recognized Jack Keudell. We didn't even know anything about the Keudells leaving Colorado. It was awfully nice to run across friends out there in the middle of nowhere.

We traveled together for several days but they were having trouble with the Model-T overheating and had to lay over. We kept going.

Charles Thompson

We landed in the Willamette Valley of Oregon, near the town of Silverton. All of us old enough to work went to pickin' berries in the fields.

On the 4th of July a parade was held in Salem. We took our covered wagon. I drove. We wrote "Oregon or Bust" on the canvas cover an' rolled up the flaps so the family could wave.

Mother refused to be in the parade. She said she didn't want to be seen with such a gypsy-looking outfit an' joined the crowd.

They put us behind a marchin' band. I had my hands full tryin' to control the horses 'cause they had never heard a marchin' band. But I recall the crowd as we passed, wavin', whistlin' an' carryin' on. I spotted Mother. She was starin' straight ahead, ignorin' us, actin' like we didn't even exist.

133

1918
HELEN KEUDELL AND BOB KEUDELL

Helen Keudell

Whenever things weren't going quite right Dad would get to figuring he could do better somewhere else. He was of a mindset that the grass was always greener down the road apiece.

I'm sure it was that feeling, or maybe a case of wanderlust, that made us leave Nebraska and head west. Not that we had much to leave; a sod house and a homestead in the Sand Hills. Our covered wagon was pulled by a mismatched team; a mule and a horse.

We traveled into Kansas. Harvest was in full swing and along the road a farmer offered Dad a job working in the fields and hired Mother to help with the cooking.

Bob Keudell

During the harvest, early one morning, Dad and the farmer went bird hunting. They came in, leaned the shotgun, a 16-gauge double-barrel, up against a wall on the porch. Dad was leery of having a loaded shotgun around and so before he went to work he broke it down.

Mother was inside cooking and the four of us kids were outside playing. Viola was nine. I was seven. Jack, five. Helen, four. Mother came to the door and called to us, "Jack and Helen, time for your nap." And then she directed Viola and me to tuck them in the bed, in the wagon. She went inside.

We were usually pretty good about doing what we were told but that day we did not. I picked up the shotgun, wanted to show I knew how to assemble it. I was holding it when it went off. I remember the noise, the smoke, the recoil tearing the shotgun loose from my grip and it clattering on the wood porch. And I remember I was scared half-to-death when I realized Jack had been shot.

Helen Keudell

Bob was monkeying with the shotgun. Jack was a little daredevil, was encouraging him, saying, "Shoot it! Shoot it!"

The gun went off. Jack's right hand just disappeared.

Mother dashed through the doorway, a dish towel over her shoulder. The screen door slammed shut. She used the dish towel as a tourniquet, tied it around the stub, all that was left of Jack's right arm. She lifted him onto the top of a pile of grain sacks that were piled on the porch and ran off to the field to where Father was working.

The three of us kids stood there in front of Jack. We were in shock, weeping and sobbing. And Jack was looking right at us. He was trying not to but big alligator tears were sliding down his cheeks and he gritted his teeth and told us, "Stop crying or you're gonna make me cry, too."

By the time harvest was over Jack was well enough to travel. But instead of continuing on in the covered wagon we loaded everything we had, including the wagon and team, in a boxcar. We came as far west as we could afford to go. That was Nampa, Idaho.

We moved into a house and Dad found a job clerking in a grocery store. I used to visit him at work and when he was busy I would sneak around back and search through the throw-away pile for something to eat. I tasted my first orange that way. So sweet and juicy, the flavor was absolutely out of this world.

Soon Dad came down with the flu. It was going around then and people were dying left and right. Dad pulled through, got well just in time to help nurse the rest of us. Mother and all of us kids came down with the flu. The doctor came over — my first introduction to a doctor — placed a thermometer under my arm, turned to Father and said, "She's got a high one, real hot fever". Dad cooked, tended house and was very determined we were all going to get well. We did.

That winter the folks corresponded with the Thompson family. We had been neighbors back in the Sand Hills of Nebraska. They were living in Loghill, Colorado, near the town of Ridgeway. They encouraged us to come down and claimed that if we did there was a place near them we could farm on shares.

Bob Keudell

The spring of 1919 we were back on the road in our covered wagon. We had the same team, the mule and the horse. We would travel along, stop at the end of the day and it might be out in the boondocks or it could be a farmer's field or a park in the middle of some small town. We didn't go through any big cities.

Mom cooked over a tin camp stove, pancakes most every meal. I had to rustle up firewood. Another of my chores was to take care of the team. They would have to be hobbled before they were turned out.

The mule had me buffaloed. If he didn't want to come in he would put up a fuss, kicking at me and trying to bite. Dad told me when he started acting up to get a switch. I tried that but the mule remained the boss.

The horse wasn't much better. He was high-strung. There were a few automobiles, very few, but when we met one the horse would be skittish, snort, throw his head and act as if he wanted to run. The mule was rock-steady and never bothered by the racing of an engine.

All of us rode in the wagon. When us kids' play turned rowdy Dad would bark at us, "Get out and walk." After a couple or three miles the fight would be forgotten and we would do most anything, make any sort of promise, to be allowed to ride again.

Helen Keudell

We moved to Loghill, on the mesa, and lived in the bunkhouse of what had been a sawmill operation. There were about a dozen families up there, including our friends the Thompsons. All of us were trying to scratch out a living but the soil was poor and the growing season very short.

We used to have community get-togethers at our place. They would toss what little furniture we had out of the way and someone would fiddle. Henry Thompson called the square dances and a bottle of bootleg whiskey would make the rounds. The adults would dance the night away. Us children, as we fell asleep, would be stacked like cordwood on one of the beds. Come morning the families would leave in their sleighs with happy faces. After they were gone, sometimes, Father and Mother would have one last dance, moving with grace and joy — no music, only the sound of shoe leather scratching against wood floors to accompany them.

Loghill was a truly beautiful place. A single valley lay between us and the Rocky Mountains. In the spring the wild crocus would come up through the melting snow and bloom in such vivid colors. There was a whole lot of crocus growing between the house and the outhouse. I would get so interested in the flowers I would barely make it to the spot I needed to go in time to avert an accident.

We lived among the mountain lions, wild cats, and bear. Every day there were wild horses to see and when they brought through flocks of sheep some would become lost. We would rescue the lambs, make them into pets. I remember Dad's annoyance after he butchered one of our lambs and us children sat at the table and cried.

"What's wrong with you?" he demanded to know.

We pointed to our plates and cried in unison, "Is this Baa?"

After two years the Thompsons moved down to the town of Montrose. We hung on through one more winter. Come spring Dad salvaged enough from selling his last wagon load of grain, our wagon, the horse and the mule, put it all down and bought a used Model-T Ford.

He never drove it home. Instead he parked it below the hill, hiding it among the trees. That night he told us, "We can't hold on any longer. We owe money to everyone in the country and there's no way we can pay 'em back. We're clearin' out."

Dad made several trips carrying the bedding and whatnot and then we took what we could carry, snuck out in the middle of the night. The only thing frivolous was the few pieces of cut glass that my mother insisted on taking. She had brought them with her when she immigrated to the United States from Germany. She treasured them so.

Bob Keudell

Everything we could carry was piled in that Model-T. On one running board was a wood box loaded with pots and pans, dishes and utensils. On the other side was another wooden box with food. We had a tent rolled up and tied on back. The four of us kids sat on boxes piled on the back seat.

There was not much of a road up and over the Rocky Mountains. We bucked snowdrifts and mud. One day we only managed to travel 30 feet. But we kept at it, a little at a time, and finally came down the western slope.

We traveled north, over dirt roads, to Idaho and followed along the south side of the Snake River. Upon reaching Oregon we were told that the roads through the mountains were especially bad and it would be a good idea to have plenty of spares. Dad bought two 30-by-3½-inch high pressure tires.

Along the way we came upon a fellow who needed a tire and Dad sold him one. We continued on and in the Blue Mountains, at a place called Emigrant Springs where the Oregon Trail wagon pioneers used to camp, we had a blowout. The tire could not be fixed with a boot so we put on the spare. A couple miles down the road another tire blew.

Dad told Mother, "I'm going to hike into Pendleton. You will have to stay here." The last thing he told her was, "We're on the Umatilla Reservation. Watch out for Indians. I'll be back when I get back."

Mother had never been around Indians and she was scared to death that we were going to get scalped before the sun came up. But we survived and late the next afternoon Dad walked into camp with a tire.

Helen Keudell

As we neared the Columbia Gorge we topped a ridge and in front of us was a covered wagon and several kids scattered along behind, walking.

Suddenly Dad let out a whoop. He hollered, "Why if it isn't that old horse trader, Henry Thompson." The wagon stopped and sure enough it was the Thompson family.

144

Babe Thompson was close to my age, we had been good friends back in Colorado. I was tired of riding on top of the boxes in the back seat of the Model-T and so to be with Babe, and also so Ralph and Jack could be together, I gave up my place and rode in the wagon.

The scenery in the Columbia Gorge was absolutely spectacular. After having come across so many miles of desert the water was bluer than blue and the forests greener than green. I saw my first wild foxgloves in bloom. When we came to patches of foxgloves Babe and I would hop off, gather a few flowers and dash to get back on the slow-moving wagon.

We hit a stretch of paved road and it was so wonderfully smooth. I sat on the rear step and bounced my feet, dragging them along the pavement.

The Model-T traveled much faster than the wagon. When we arrived at the evening camp the folks had a fire going and dinner was almost ready. I walked over toward the campfire and Dad noticed right away, demanded to know, "What have you done to your shoes?"

I answered very sheepishly, "I guess I wore them out."

"How did you manage that?"

"From dragging my feet on the pavement."

"I didn't pay good money for those shoes to have you treat them like that. You'll go barefooted the rest of the summer." And I did.

Bob Keudell

We were running low on money for groceries and having trouble with the Model-T overheating. We stopped near the town of Troutdale, at Clyde LaFollette's farm. Mother and us kids picked loganberries, Dad hauled berries to the cannery at Fairview.

It was chilly the morning of July 19th. I was sitting close to the cook stove in order to warm myself. Mother had a big pot of coffee perking on the back of the stove. She was busy cooking pancakes. I don't know how it happened other than Mother reached for something, knocked the coffee pot over in my lap. Scalding hot coffee burned me. I screamed in pain, dreadful pain.

Making it even worse — I was wearing long underwear and so, of course, that held in the heat and cooked my leg all the more. Had I only been wearing loose trousers it would not have burned so deeply.

Right after my accident Mother went into shock. On July 22 Dad came to the hospital where I had been taken, whispered to me, "I'm sorry, but your mother is dead." I didn't cry right then but I did later on, after he had gone.

Mother was buried in a pauper's grave at the Multnomah County Cemetery on 82nd Street in Portland. They kept me in the hospital for six long months.

Helen Keudell

Before Dad took Mother to the hospital I can remember her kissing each of us and saying, "Now you be good kids." That was the last any of us saw of her. I am glad I never went to the funeral because it would have clung to my mind if I had seen her in a casket. This way I can remember her kissing me good-by.

Dad came home from the hospital. He gathered us around. "Your momma is ... you don't have a momma anymore."

The farmer's wife where we were staying, Lewella LaFollette, took me into her house. She shampooed my hair, gave me a bath and baked me a cake. It was my birthday.

146

1918
MICK BREWER

ad was superintendent of one of the coal mines in Colorado but he gave up on that and decided to be a farmer. We loaded two covered wagons and headed to Wyoming.

Wyoming wasn't all it was cracked up to be and so we ended up renting a boxcar and bringing our outfits as far as Lewiston, Idaho. From there we headed west into Oregon, following along the Columbia River.

There were seven of us kids in the family. In order to feed us all Dad and some of the older boys, I was only six, would find work at farms here and there.

In one of the towns we passed through somebody made mention that Corvallis, Oregon was a booming place, lots of sawmills and jobs a dime a dozen. So we went there and Dad caught on pulling green chain in a mill.

But it rained too much in Corvallis and Dad said if we stayed he was gonna rust. So we hitched up the team, started for Montana. Dad had heard good things said about Montana.

We crossed the Cascade Mountains over Santiam Pass and got caught in the middle of a snowstorm. The higher we went the more it snowed. We had a cook stove in one of the wagons and Mother kept a fire goin'. It was nice and warm in there. That was where us kids rode.

The snow got so deep we had to leave one wagon and double-hitch our teams. We came down out of the mountains and the sun was shining to where you couldn't hardly believe there was a blizzard on top. We camped on the outskirts of the town of Sisters. Next day Dad took all the horses, went back and brought the other wagon through.

We started out across the desert. I remember we came to a homestead with the house on one side of the road and the barn on the other. Chickens scattered in between. I was powerful hungry for chicken. So I got out the fish line, worked a kernel of corn onto the hook, threw out a handful of corn and my bait, too.

A big rooster picked it up. I let him get it down in his gullet and set the hook, reeled in the line hand over hand quick-like so he wouldn't squawk none, and I wring his neck.

That evening when we pulled up to camp, I drug out my rooster. Dad, he wasn't none too pleased. But one thing about Dad — he was a practical man. We had chicken for dinner. Best chicken dinner I ever 'et.

150

1921
ALBERT DAVIS

reat-Grandmother came to Oregon in a covered wagon pulled by oxen. Along Snake River, at Farewell Bend, she gave birth to my grandfather. The only other thing I know about their trip was that the wagon train was attacked by Indians and several of the pioneers were killed.

My Oregon Trail experience was a bit tamer. I'll get to that after I tell about living in Milton, Oregon. We had a nice home there and Dad made a living with horses; hauling freight, making grocery deliveries, building roads for the county, running a water wagon on the streets to keep the dust down. He done some construction work, too.

Dad was a Percheron man, said they were the hardest-working animal on the face of the earth. His weakness was for iron grays. He had iron grays almost exclusively.

153

Dad was a hard-working man, bit of a dreamer, too. During World War I he read literature about big money being made growing wheat in Montana. He got it in his head to move to Montana. Said we were gonna get rich raising wheat. Mother wasn't too thrilled at the prospects but went along with him anyway. That was the kind of woman she was.

Come the first sign of spring Dad rented a boxcar. He was gonna take the horses and other animals and our belongings to Montana. Mother was to stay with us, there were six children, while we finished school. And then we were to rejoin him.

I had a little black shepherd, a cow dog really, name of Jack. You know how kids are hard to get out of bed in the morning. Mom would open the bedroom door, tell Jack, "Wake him up," and Jack would come after me, jump on the bed, and even if I went under the covers his cold, wet nose would root me out and he would lick my face, pester me until I had no choice but to get up and go to school.

On the day Dad pulled out in the boxcar he was going to take Jack with him. But the depot agent came along, said a health inspection slip had to be filled out before he could allow the dog on board. He claimed the only place such a slip could be obtained was thirty miles away in Pendleton. There was no time for that and no way we could bring him when we traveled on the train as passengers. Dad said I would have to give him away.

I remember sitting there, tears rolling down my cheeks, and that agent came by, put his hand on my shoulder and told me, "Son, I've got to run into my office. Whatever is in that boxcar when I get back is going." I knew what he meant, slipped Jack through the open door and that was it.

One end of the boxcar was loaded with furniture and personal belongings and our wagon and two-seat buggy. The other end held four horses, a milk cow and chickens in a cage. Jack slept with Dad on a bed he had fixed up in the wagon box.

Dad wrote from Montana that the trip had gone without so much as a single hitch. He milked the cow, gave milk and eggs to the crew and they invited him to eat with them in the caboose.

The day after school let out we took the passenger train to Columbus, Montana. Dad met us with the wagon and all six of us kids crowded in back among the suitcases. When we reached the farm Dad pulled up in front of a little old one-room log cabin. Mother sat there and dabbed at her eyes with the tail of a scarf.

When we lived in Milton we had a telephone, running water in the house and electricity. Although the only electrical appliance Mother had was an iron, it meant a lot to her. She brought it along to Montana but it was evident she wasn't going to be able to use it.

Finally she dried her eyes, turned to Father and told him, "Ed, if I had the money I would buy these kids tickets and take them home."

As far as I know that was the last she said about going back to Oregon. That matter eventually took care of itself.

The first year we got caught in a drought. The second it looked like we would bring in a crop but just before harvest a hailstorm hit, knocked the grain from the sheath and laid everything flat. We simply starved out.

That was in '21. The folks held an auction and sold everything except the horses, the wagons, the cook stove and our personal belongings. After paying our bills Dad said he figured we had just enough left over to buy groceries and horse feed back to Oregon.

We made ready to leave Montana. Dad built a board-and-batten shack on one the wagons. It was sixteen-foot long and eight-foot wide. Outside he wrapped it with tar paper and inside was nothing but stud walls. The wood stove, it was a Kitchen Queen and Mother's pride and joy, was bolted to the floor. And there were cupboards, a table and some chairs and a bed in the back. We called it the cook van.

Another thing we did was to butcher a couple hogs and load them in brine. And we butchered three dozen chickens, Mom canned them in half-gallon Mason jars.

We pulled out. Dad drove the cook van, the door propped open to give him room, sitting in a kitchen chair. My oldest brother, Otha, drove the covered wagon. I rode with him and we pulled a trail wagon loaded with the two hogs on brine, feed for the horses and a cage of banty chickens that belonged to me. And Jack, he ran along beside or hitched a ride when he could.

Grandfather Davis, Dad's father — we called him Grandpa Charley, came along. He was an old man. He drove a buggy with chev, which means he drove a single horse.

Within a few days we had everything lined out and going our way. Dad and Mom slept on the bed in the cook van and my sister and the two young-uns slept on the floor. Grandpa Charley slept on the ground under the van. Otha and Gilbert and I slept in the covered wagon.

Of the morning Mom would be up early, have a fire going, the van warm and breakfast cooking. And in the evening, even before we stopped, she would start the fire and be preparing dinner, peeling spuds and the like, whatever she could manage to do in the herky, jerky wagon.

Every few days Mother would get out the tubs, heat water and wash clothes on a scrub board. She brought along a clothes line. One end would be fastened to the cook van and the other to whatever was handy, a tree, a rock, the covered wagon.

We were planning on crossing the Rocky Mountains through Teton Pass. It was one of the highest, if not the highest, wagon road in North America. We made it to Livingston and the ranger held us up, said it was too late in the fall, said if a storm caught us, with all the kids, some were gonna die.

We waited a day or two, the ranger received a favorable weather report and he allowed us to pass on the condition that when we reached the other side we telephone and let him know we made it.

Going through we traveled from sunup until sundown. The road followed along the railroad grade and we passed time waving to the engineers and they always waved back.

This one time we had stopped beside a small stream and were carrying buckets to water the horses. The train came chugging up the grade and that chug-chug-chug was so loud and clear in the cold mountain air. Just when the engine reached us the engineer, wishing us good luck or calling out howdy, blew his whistle. Oh, it was loud! Any other horses would have run away, but not our horses.

On the wagons we had seven iron grays and a bay. There was Prince and Fanny, Patsy and Eagle, Dan and Dazzle, Bird and the bay. I can't recall the name of the bay.

The entire way the sky was blue and not a single flake of snow fell on us, but it was cold and blustery. We came to the little town of Yellowstone and Dad telephoned the ranger to let him know we made it.

We dropped down out of the mountains to the Snake River. It was a big river. But back on Teton Pass I saw where it started from a little lake, and I stood straddle of the outlet. That day we crossed the stream seventeen times, each time it got a little bigger and a little bigger.

We followed along the Snake and as it turned west we picked up the Oregon Trail. It was nothing more than ruts that crossed and recrossed our gravel road and sometimes we traveled over the top of it.

There were a lot of small towns scattered along through that country. And it seemed like every time we came to a settlement my banty rooster, he was in a cage on top of the feed box in the trail wagon, would commence crowing. It used to embarrass the heck out of my brother. He even tried covering over the cage with a tarp before we came to a town but somehow that rooster knew. "Cock-a-doodle-do! Cock-a-doodle-do!" Otha threatened to ring his neck. I just laughed at him.

We must have been a sight for sore eyes because several times newspaper reporters stopped us and asked if they could take a picture of our outfit. They would want to know where we were coming from, where we were going and some of the particulars. I remember one of them said we might be the last covered wagon over the Oregon Trail.

Near the town of Kimberly, Idaho it snowed on us. Dad figured that was as good a spot as any to winter over. He found us a house and us kids started school, driving back and forth to Hansen in the trail wagon.

If you had set Dad down in the middle of the Sahara Desert he could have found work. He and Otha got jobs at a gravel pit near Hansen, loading out and hauling gravel.

That winter I lost Jack. Like I said before, Jack and I were pretty much inseparable. He was as smart as dogs get. Back in Montana we turned our milk cows out to graze. There weren't any fences in that country. They would get mixed in with some of the cattle Miller & Lux had on open range. I would tell Jack, "Get the cows," and he would separate ours from the others. One time I had a rider from Miller & Lux offer me the pick of any two-year-old heifer in exchange for Jack. I told him I wouldn't trade even if he gave me the whole herd.

Jack flat disappeared into thin air. I thought maybe he might have stepped in a trap and I traveled all over the country, inquiring of the neighbors if they had seen him. But none had. What I figured was he liked Montana better than Idaho and he had headed for home.

Come spring we started west again. We were on dirt roads and gravel roads, pretty much following the way the emigrants had come over the Oregon Trail.

We didn't see many automobiles but we saw a few. At one point a fellow in a Studebaker touring car passed us and pulled back in. With all the dust I guess he failed to see the cook van because he ran smack-dab into the back of it. Never did any damage to the van but punched a hole in his radiator.

Dad felt the jolt, stopped and came back to inspect the damage. The fellow climbed out of the Studebaker. He was dressed in nice clothes and it was plain to see he wasn't a working stiff. It was also pretty evident he had been drinking. In fact, he was drunker than a hoot owl.

"What am I going to do? Oh, what am I going to do?" he wailed, wringing his hands.

Dad told him, "I'll tow you to town."

And that was what we did. The driver sat there steering and taking pulls on the moonshine jug. When we reached town he gave Dad five dollars. Dad refused it but the fellow insisted.

We made it almost to the Oregon border and got waylaid. They were building a railroad, needed men and teams to work and hired Dad, Otha and me. They gave Grandpa Charley handwork with a shovel. And for seventy-five cents a day my younger brother Gilbert rode a horse and delivered water bags to the working men.

That was my first job at a man's pay. I was 14 and ran a fresno. Don't ask me how I done it; a man can hold the lines in one hand and work the Johnson bar with the other but I only went a hundred pounds if I was soaking wet. I would hold the reins with both hands and somehow manage to trip the bar. I done 'er but don't know how. Worked ten hours a day, seven days a week.

We were camped there in the sagebrush and sand from May to September and finally it came to the point where if we waited any longer we were going to have to spend the winter. And so we hit the trail.

Grandpa Charley had spent a few days in Bend, Oregon. He told what a bustling town it was with two mills operating, Shevlin-Hixon and Brooks-Scanlon. He said it was a good place to settle and that there would be plenty of work for us. And so that was the direction we headed, out across eastern Oregon on the route of Stephen Meek's Lost Wagon Train.

They came through in 1845, ran short on water and suffered terribly. We too ran low on water and Grandpa Charley would drive his buggy ahead and try to locate water and a place for us to camp of the night. One time he found a nice spring but Dad said we were going to go on and try to get a few more miles under our belt. Grandpa was mad. He said, "No use for me to find a spot if you ain't gonna stop there." We went on and that night had to make dry camp.

We ran into some bad luck near Wagontire Mountain. The van was in front, going out across the desert, when all of a sudden it flopped over on its side. Happened just that quick, wheels on the left side both hit chuckholes and she turned turtle. Dad managed to jump free but Mom and my youngest brother, Glen, were inside. The way they screamed and carried on I was scared to death they were dying. Dad, he couldn't turn loose of the horses or else we were going to have more of a mess on our hands than we already had; so I jumped down, opened up the back door to the cook van. The bed and all the boxes stored under it had come over on Mom and Glen. I managed to pull them out. They weren't hurt a bit.

We dug out the log chains, fastened one end to the running gear and took them over the top of the van, had the horses pull the wagon upright. I don't know how we kept the wheels from caving in but everything held and before long we were back on the road no worse for wear.

The Cascade Mountains, with a coating of fresh snow, were visible a long ways out. We kept coming and set camp outside Bend on the south side of Pilot Butte. There was an irrigation ditch and plenty of water for drinking and the stock.

The first night we were there five or six cars loaded with Willamette Valley deer hunters camped near us. The had a big bonfire and were drinking moonshine from a jug they passed around. There was singing and loud voices. Dad told us to stay away from their camp. He wasn't a drinking man but Grandpa Charley paid them a visit. Grandpa Charley always did like the nectar.

We camped there until Dad found us a place to settle. It was a little farm at Tumalo. And that was it. **Our roaming** days were over.

Left to right: Edwin Sells, Rena Sells and Erma Sells, Anna Osborne and Billy Osborne.

ACKNOWLEDGEMENTS

With special thanks to the pioneers and their families for sharing their stories.

EPILOGUE

George Craig — 1889

George Craig was born October 18, 1883 in Scotts Bluff, Nebraska. The family included father Chester, mother Lydia and sister Jane.

Chester ran a stage line to support the family but when he found one of his stages with the driver and passenger frozen and the four-mule team dead, still standing in the traces, he decided to look for a home in a more tempered climate.

The Craigs started west in 1889 and settled on an eighty-acre homestead near Bremerton, Washington. The following year they returned to Nebraska. Their second trip west began in 1899. After the wagon accident in the Blue Mountains they returned to the last valley they had passed, the Grand Ronde Valley, and settled there.

George logged and farmed. He married Lulu Dott. After more than sixty years of marriage she died and George moved to the Twin Fir retirement home in LaGrande. He died in 1979.

Pages 14-19

Clifton Ross — 1891

Clifton Ross was born September 29, 1881 and crossed from Nebraska to Brownsville, Oregon in 1891 with his father, John Wesley, mother, Buelah, an older brother and an aunt. The top buggy that was such a novelty crossing the Oregon Trail was sold after they reached the Willamette Valley.

Clifton worked cutting firewood, farming and was employed for 35 years as a rural route mail carrier for the United States Postal Service.

In 1908 Clifton married Carrie Prince. They had two children, Milo and Doryce. They lived for many years at the Friendsview Manor in Newberg, Oregon. Carrie died in March of 1980. Clifton died in October of 1980, shortly after celebrating his 99th birthday.

Pages 20-23

Grace Byers (Thogerson) — 1892

Grace Byers was born October 18, 1888 in Battle Creek, Nebraska. The Byers family included father Rolla, mother Lillie and brother Arthur, who was four years older than Grace. They departed from Nebraska headed for Hillsboro, Oregon in 1892.

Grace married John Thogerson in 1911 and they had four children. They bought property on Center Ridge, south of The Dalles, Oregon, and farmed.

John died in 1973 and Grace died in 1981. They are buried in Vancouver, Washington beside their youngest child, Donny, who died of pneumonia when he was five years old.

Pages 24-27

Zola Lawrence (Menear) — 1896

Zola Lawrence was born October 28, 1892 in Goodland, Kansas. The Lawrence family included father John, mother Della and Percy, a brother one year younger than Zola. They came to Oregon in 1896. Accompanying them were grandparents Billy and Ellen Lawrence and two uncles and a friend.

Zola married logger Wayne Menear in 1911. He was severely injured in a woods accident by a widow maker and was never able to return to working in the woods. He died in 1964 at the age of 76. Zola is a resident at Cascade Manor in Lebanon, Oregon.

Pages 28-31

Mabel Jones (Myles) — 1898

Mabel Jones was born June 20, 1890 in Hayes County, Nebraska. The Jones family included father Jackson, mother Lydia, sisters Lilly and Leolah and brothers Alma, Lawrence, Jack and Charley.

Jackson was a gypsy horse trader, never satisfied unless on the move. In 1898 he heard of good land available near Sunnyside, Washington and they departed Nebraska.

On the 4th day of August they landed in North Powder, Oregon and that was where they stuck. Twice Jackson tried to return the family to Nebraska. The first time they reached the Snake River but when Alma's daughter nearly drowned they took it as an omen and returned to North Powder. The second time, in 1921, Jackson was stopped by a stroke and for the rest of his days he talked about how happy he had been with reins in his hands and a hill in front of him.

Mabel was content in North Powder. She met farmer George Myles at a "kitchen sweat" dance and they married in 1906. George died in 1953. Mabel died in 1984.

Pages 32-35

Minnie Pfannebecker (Gill) — 1898

Minnie Pfannebecker was born February 14, 1895. At the age of three she came west from Buffalo, Missouri with her parents, brothers Harry and Ed, and sisters Nanny and Ella. The horse Minnie loved so much, Dick, lived to be 27 years old before being destroyed.

Minnie married Harry Gill in 1928 and they farmed near Big Butte on the prairie outside Grangeville, Idaho. They had four children, Marjorie, Richard, Dale and Glen.

In 1973 Minnie returned to Montpelier, Idaho with her sisters Nanny and Ella. They checked all the old barns looking in vain for the wagon that had been parked there so many years before and the doll that had accidently been left behind.

Harry died in 1982. Minnie died in 1990.

Pages 36-41

Bertha "Bird" Shadley (McCoy) — 1900

Bird Shadley was born April 29, 1896 in Clear Creek, California. At the time of their departure from California the family included father Abe, mother Belle, and sisters Ethel and Minnie.

As far as her nickname goes Bird does not know how it originated except to say, "When I was a baby I must have chirped like a bird."

Bird married Clarence McCoy in 1918. He taught high school for many years and then became an orchardist, growing pears. They had three children, Evelyn, Mariam and Willa. Clarence died in 1957.

Bird lived in Hood River County, Oregon for 70 years. She recently moved to Burns, Oregon to be near her grandchildren and great-grandchildren.

Pages 44-53

Lola Kennedy (Culver) and George Kennedy — 1900

Lola Kennedy was born October 31, 1887. George Kennedy was born November 1, 1889. The Kennedy family consisted of father William, mother Ora Bell and six children. They came to Oregon in 1900.

Lola was married to Earl Culver for 37 years. He was a logger and farmer. Lola died in LaGrande, Oregon in 1986 and is buried in the Elgin cemetery.

The Kennedys were bringing Florence, the horse that kicked and broke George's jaw, west for a family friend, Lucy Scott. Lucy promised George she would name one of her children after him and she did, naming her second child, a girl, Georgia.

George spent years roaming the country but returned to Elgin, Oregon and began courting Georgia. One day they were sitting on a stump and George was rolling a dice in his hand. He told Georgia he would marry her if it came up a six spot, and it did.

For years George and Georgia would roll that dice to settle any argument. After Georgia died George took the dice with the rounded corners and gave it to a couple who had recently married. He told them, "Any little argument starts, chuck the dice, high man wins."

George died in 1985.

Pages 54-65

Florence Boggs (Horn) — 1903

Florence Boggs was born June 25, 1897 in Woodburn, Oregon. The Boggs family included father Thomas, mother Lizzie and brothers Howard and Lester.

Florence married Clinton Chorpening. They had three children, Glen, Clinton and Clarice. They were divorced after 12 years of marriage. With her children Florence moved to Bonanza, Oregon and operated a drug store.

The drug store was next to the Bank of Bonanza and in 1932 Florence married the bank president, John Horn. They had one child, Jack. John died in 1952. Florence continues to live in her home beside Big Springs Park in Bonanza, Oregon.

Pages 66-75

Sedalia Rucker (Dexter) — 1906

Sedalia Rucker was born December 2, 1892 in Wallowa, Oregon. Her mother Lucinda died of typhoid in 1894 and her father died three years later. Five-year-old Sedalia was taken in and reared by Lew and Ella Rinehart.

In 1906 they crossed Oregon over the Oregon Trail and settled on a farm in Yamhill County. Not long after they arrived Sedalia was involved in an accident with wild horses. One leg was crushed and was later amputated.

Sedalia married her sweetheart Bert Dexter in 1910. In 1924 they again loaded a wagon with their belongings and moved to Umatilla, Oregon. They parked the wagon behind the barn and it eventually rotted away and the team of workhorses died of old age. Sedalia died in 1984.

Pages 76-81

Maude Mosier (Longacre) — 1912

Maude Mosier was born March 16, 1893 near Mt. Ayr, Iowa. The Mosier family who came west in 1912 included father John, mother Emma, brothers Archie and Bert and grandfather Abraham.

In 1913 Maude returned to Nebraska by train. Her boyfriend, Daniel Webster (Web) Longacre, had built a home and a barn on his homestead. He proposed to her immediately but it was not until 1915 that Maude agreed to marry him. They farmed and four children were born, one boy and three girls.

To avoid the cold winters of the plains they moved to the southern Oregon coast in 1946 and began raising lilies. Web died in 1956. Maude resides north of Brookings at the end of Longacre Road and is cared for by her daughter Iola Mullen.

Page 82-97

Irma Sells (Hopkins) — 1913

Irma Sells, born August 13, 1902 at South Omaha, Nebraska, was the only child of Edwin and Rena. Their traveling companions on the wagon trip west were Billy and Anna Osborne. What became of the Osbornes is unknown.

After the wagon trip to California the Sells family returned to South Omaha where they operated a grocery store on 41st and Hamilton Streets. Edwin and Rena eventually divorced.

Irma married Charles Freyer in 1923. He drove ice truck. They had three sons, Wesley, Dale and Donald. Charles died in 1965. Irma remarried Fred Hopkins in 1967. Fred died in 1977.

Irma is a resident of Bethesda Care Center in Ashland, Nebraska.

Pages 98-117

Charles Thompson and Ralph Thompson — 1915

The Thompson family included father Henry, mother Ethel and their children Elzie, Freida, Charles and Ralph. The family eventually settled in California. Henry died in 1960 and Ethel died in 1962.

Charles was born September 10, 1908 in Des Moines, Iowa. He worked at various jobs including farming, logging and lumber millwork. He married Relda in 1934 and they had three children, Ethel, Jack and Barbara. For a number of years Charles operated the Ukiah Trading Post in Ukiah, California and later the Acme Saw Shop in Sacramento, California. Charles and Relda reside in Sacramento, California.

Ralph was born two months premature on March 19, 1911 on the homestead near Valentine, Nebraska. He related, "When I was born the doctor figured I was a lost cause and was trying to save Mother. She was in pretty bad shape. Dad took me, wrapped me up in some cotton, put me in a shoe box on the open oven door of the wood stove. Dad said he was bound and determined to save me and he did."

As a young man Ralph worked as a plumber, surveyor, farmer, heavy equipment operator and he had a 31-year-career as a pipe fitter and lead mechanic for Standard Oil. The eye that was injured when he was a boy has been removed. He lives in Pine Grove, California.

Pages 118-133

Helen Keudell (Jones) and Bob Keudell — 1918

The Keudell family included father John, mother Mary and their children Viola, born in 1908, and Bob, born in 1910, in a sod house near Braden, Nebraska; and Jack, born in 1912, and Helen, born in 1914, in Lewellyn, Nebraska.

Mary died in 1922. In 1927 John remarried Edna May Woosley and they had eight children, five boys and three girls. Viola married Arnold White in 1925 and they had two daughters. Viola died in 1966. Jack married Muriel Bowen and they had three sons. Jack owned the Pontiac and GMC dealership in St. Helens, Oregon. He died in 1971.

Bob worked his way through high school and college, earning a degree in electrical engineering from Oregon State University. He enjoyed a long career as an electrical engineer with Portland General Electric. He married Jennie Lindros in 1938 and they had two children, Barbara and Robert Alan. Bob and Jennie reside in Salem, Oregon.

Helen worked her way through high school and three years at Willamette University before marrying Malcolm Jones in 1936. Helen worked as a portrait painter for Hise Studio in Corvallis for 25 years. Malcolm worked for 38 years as an attorney for the Oregon Public Utility Commission. They had one son, Malcolm Lundy, Jr. Helen and Malcolm reside in Salem, Oregon.

Pages 134-147

Mick Brewer — 1918

Mick Brewer was born October 24, 1912 at Fort Lupton, Colorado. The Brewer family included father Edward, mother Lotty and brothers and sisters Bus (Edward, Jr.), Billy, Jim, Bessie, Jess and Fred.

Mick married Dolly Brethauer in 1933 and they had three daughters, Betty, Dolly, and Ruth. Mick farmed in Colorado until World War II when he worked in the shipyards in Portland. In 1943 he began working in the woods for Ochoco Lumber Company and he worked there until he retired in 1973. He lives with Dolly in Prineville, Oregon. Jim Brewer lives in Paonia, Colorado. Jess Brewer lives in Dolan Springs, Arizona. Bessie Brewer (Coats) lives in Crawford, Colorado.

Pages 148-151

Albert Davis — 1921

Albert Davis was born October 20, 1907 at Milton, Oregon. At the time the Davis family returned to Oregon by wagon from Montana the family included father Ed, mother Bessie, brothers and sisters Otha, Lucille, Gilbert, Merle and Glen and grandfather Charley Davis. The family settled on a small farm near Tumalo, Oregon. In 1926 they once again loaded the wagons and cook van and journeyed to Umatilla County, Oregon where they settled in Weston and began farming.

Albert returned to central Oregon in 1931. He married Marie in 1945. They ranched near Dry Creek and later near Powell Butte, Oregon. Marie died in 1988. Albert resides in Prineville, Oregon.

Pages 152-167

1918 Brewer Family.